ENTANGLED

A Woman's Guide
to Recognizing Your Emotional Affair
and Restoring Your Marriage

AMY J. BENNETT

Entangled
Amy J. Bennett
© 2011 All Rights Reserved
All Scripture quotations, unless otherwise indicated, are taken from the New
International Version 1984.
Scripture quotations marked KJV are from the King James Version.
Scripture quotations marked MSG are from The Message.
ISBN 978-1467910255
EntangledBook.com
Cover design melissaoyler.com

Contents

Introduction

On a recent October afternoon, my coworkers and I were headed to a corn maze, and I was legitimately scared I was going to get lost. I could just imagine retracing the same path countless times, never finding a way out, calling for help and no one answering. I was sure I'd be spending the night in the gloppy mud between spindly stalks of corn. OK, maybe that is a bit dramatic. It turns out the owner stands on a bridge and all I would have to do is raise a flag, which had been given to me at the start line, and he would lead me out. But it got me thinking about life. Sometimes we enter paths we don't want to follow; some of the same ones over and over, all leading to dead ends. We don't know how to get out. At some point we have to raise our flags and ask for directions.

A few years ago, I headed down paths I never thought I'd find myself on. At times, it all felt like a fun game, and I was content to lose myself in the maze. But when I finally wanted out, I realized I was stuck. I kept retracing my steps because what should have felt like the wrong way had quickly become familiar. In just a few short weeks six years ago, I found myself emotionally checked out of my marriage and checked in with a person with whom I worked. I wondered if I had missed my real soul mate. I was sure I had found the real fairy tale I'd been looking for all my life. I was having secret conversations, dreaming about a guy who wasn't my husband and wondering how I got there. And night after night, I found myself lying in the mud not willing to raise a flag for help.

God finally found me in the mud and mire and through his spectacular grace led me out of the entangled mess I had put myself in.

Maybe you know how it feels to question your husband and your marriage. Maybe you know how it feels to have feelings for someone else. Maybe you know how it feels to hide your text messages and Facebook account because if your spouse saw it, you'd be mortified and just a little afraid you'd lose everything. I've been there. Lost in the middle of the cornfield.

I know it's scary and confusing right now. This book is my attempt to shout from a bull horn on a bridge to the middle of the field where you are and give you the directions out. Because there is a way out. But some of it is not easy. The path out is bumpy and even painful at times but I can tell you how good the freedom feels when you find your way out.

So will you walk with me? I need to tell you about a time I got lost in a cornfield.

SECTION I

THE ENTANGLING

Section I is the story of how I got lost in the maze. It's this outward confession that gives the rest of the book legs on which to stand.

2.5

2.5. An acquaintance called me that once. 2.5? My brain scanned for possible meanings. Are we rating my outfit? Hair? IQ? What? 2.5 was an awfully low number on nearly every scale I imagined. As a Type A first-born child, I wasn't accustomed to a 2.5 anything. "Sure, you're very 2.5," he explained, "You know, married, picket fence, 2.5 kids." I thought of my husband, two girls, chocolate lab, and picket fence at my suburban home. "Yeah, I guess I am." Very 2.5. In fact, I'd always been very 2.5.

You may remember, as a child, being asked to describe yourself using the first letter of your first name. Fittingly enough, Amy was the "A" student. And also "Angel". Yes. 2.5.

I started my own faith journey, asking Jesus into my heart, in a little church service being held in a house while I was just in grade school. Some Christian folk have the exact date written somewhere but for one, I don't recall our little ministry church having too much in the way of Sunday School supplies. In fact, classes were held on the beds of the ladies living there. Plus, we were Pentecostal. I got saved more times than I can count.

I easily managed to stay on the straight and narrow through school, a little out of fear that I'd lose my salvation and a lot because I loved Jesus. My first-born tendencies coupled with my spiritualized little life meant that I was pretty sure I had planned my 2.5 days by the time I was 11. With God's blessing, of course. In fact, I met my husband at 15 and was married only 2 weeks after I turned 20, during the summer between my sophomore and junior years of college. I went on to earn my Computer Science honors degree, and just a week after my college graduation we got a chocolate lab named Mattie. You know, the practice-for-a-child puppy.

By age 25, I was working full time at a bank, where I had always dreamed of working, and we'd had our first daughter Emma. We had struggled to conceive for more than a year, having wanted to start a family as soon as I got out of college. She was the first grandchild for my parents and the first girl for my in-laws. To say she was treasured is quite the understatement.

My husband, Scott, got his dream job on the Highway Patrol the same fall we had Emma. He was off to police academy for 6 months when she was only 7 weeks old. That summer after he graduated from the academy we moved an hour away from our support system. We stayed only a year before asking for a transfer back home as I was pregnant with our second daughter, Lexi. We moved into our house in the suburbs of Charlotte where the 2.5 picket fence still stands. Everything was going as planned. Or so it seemed.

What no one could see, was that within that 2.5 picket fence and inside our little home, we were becoming anything but 2.5. Satan had been at work in our lives; I could feel the arrows but I never saw the destruction coming. A year later we were hit with a full-on attack against our family that threatened to shatter our 2.5 into shards of piercing glass.

Chinks

Theme Song:
Mine, Taylor Swift

Through the years, my husband has become well known for his particular ways. He's orderly. Neat. Organized. Structured. His job as a state trooper suits him well. He gets to find things that are wrong and make people pay for them. He's been a trooper for 9 of the 17 years I've known him and I can say with assurance that in addition to our family, his job brings him ultimate happiness. Order is his drug of choice.

When we first married, it was a point of contention if I left the cabinet doors open in the kitchen. He was constantly closing them behind me and requesting I do the same. My water glasses, left in the living room or kitchen counter, had a peculiar way of disappearing before I'd had more than a couple of sips. If an object was sitting out of place and Scott spotted it, he was certain to put it back. As a new homemaker, this worked out well for me. I'd leave something out and sure enough, it would disappear back to its original spot.

What I didn't realize is just how much all this out-of-place stuff bothered him. His quirks became a running joke to visiting friends. At times, people would move a chair over just a few inches to glean a reaction. While Scott insisted it didn't bother him, I knew without fail the chair would be fixed before we went to bed.

To no fault of our girls, after they were born I was still working from home and it became impossible for me to keep up with both their needs and work demands. I exhausted myself by continually picking up the onslaught of onesies, blankies, bottles, diapers and toys, but it wasn't enough. His irritation of out-of-place things began to boil to the point of anger.

He would enter the house, see a few toys in the living room floor, and he'd go into a tirade about the disaster. Disaster to him seemed to mean just a few things out of place, and my feelings would be intensely hurt. I was doing the best I could. His verbal onslaught would cause me to shut down. I found myself not wanting to kiss him hello. My lack of greeting would leave him feeling unloved. This would begin the evening's downward spiral. His irritation about the living room would spill into every conversation we had. He had a smart-aleck response to everything I said and I in return could give him nothing more than a smart-aleck response. I am not innocent. I did not respond well to the attacks.

We'd been through enough marriage books and sessions to know how important it is to remain physically connected. Even if we were in a bad cycle, we'd continue to be intimate. It was usually on those tense, silent evenings we'd finally have to break the ice and rehash the same argument so we could be pleasant enough to be intimate.

During those discussions, Scott always admitted where he was wrong, apologized and promised to be better. I would also commit to encouraging him better and showing him more physical affection when he walked through the door. And he would for a time, but it always seemed like his need for things to be in their place always overwhelmed whatever desire he had to keep his word.

I don't mean to impress that he was mentally abusive or even a bad husband or father. He is and has always been amazing. He's good — so good — with our girls. He often bends over backward to make sure I get what I desire. He's great about helping around the house, complimenting me, bringing me small gifts after work and doing just about anything I ask of him.

But during that time, we always were in a vicious cycle. He would blow up, I would shut down. He would feel unloved and lash out more and I would shut down more.

The summer after Lexi was born, I remember my mom asked how we were doing. I'm not sure if she could tell we weren't being pleasant or it was just her way of checking in. I remember crying into the phone, confessing to her, "I just wish he'd be nice to me."

We were entering our seventh year of marriage, infamously referred to as a challenging one, and with a nursing baby and a 2-year-old underfoot, well, things were just ripe for being tough.

Deception Point

Theme Song:

Slow Fade, Casting Crowns

"Could you do me a favor?" I typed in a chat to a coworker.

"Sure," came his instant reply. I didn't expect anything different. We had been on the same IT development team at a large bank for a year or so but had recently been teamed up to work on some projects together. During the past few months, we'd been chatting quite a bit and I'd found that we got along well. But he was nice to everyone. As a computer programmer, I was accustomed to always being the only female on the team and hadn't thought anything of our frequent chats.

"If I email something, will you print it and fax it for me?" I was working from home full time and didn't have access to a fax machine. My endorsed monthly time sheets needed to be turned in to my contracting company.

"Sure," came back his seemingly standard reply.

"Sent." I typed into the instant messaging box after sending the email.

A few minutes passed and I received a message alert.

"Sent," he'd said back.

"Thanks so much. That really saved me."

"Anything for my Amy."

I had to read his message twice. I could feel my heartbeat skip and my face flush as I understood his possessive tone. That was the first time he'd ever said anything so ... personal. While we had talked a lot during the months prior, this was the first time it had any sort of flirtatious tone. I replied back with a smiley face, not sure what else to say. But to be honest, I was flattered. We'd worked together for more than a year but we'd been chatting a lot during the past few weeks. A friendship had blossomed out of nowhere. And with charming statements like that, what was a girl supposed to think?

I didn't have time to decide what to make of all that because Scott was coming home with his standard greeting. "Wow, when did a tornado come through the house?" Scott surveyed the living room, staring down the misplaced blanket with several stuffed animals on it, some books and a few chairs. He made his way to the kitchen to put his work stuff in its place. I quickly closed the chat session on my work laptop and tried to explain the mess. "I had an hour-long conference call and the girls were playing school." All the while my heart, which had been building walls against these slings and arrows from Scott, was now racing, wondering just what the guy on the other end of the laptop was going to say next.

During the next week we continued our flirtatious conversations, each talk becoming more intimate than the last. He was overly complimentary about my looks, clothes and character. Compliments turned into deep discussions about dreams and issues. I had heard he had converted from Christianity to Judaism, which inspired many spiritual conversations. I was always sharing stories and struggles relating to my children. We clicked more. And more. And even when we did not agree, we had healthy discussions. Healthy discussions were something Scott and I rarely had. Scott is a black-and-white kind of guy; and if you can imagine, one doesn't have discussions as much as one listens to speeches on Scott's viewpoint.

Then, the real trouble began. We got along so well we couldn't help but wonder what it would have been like to meet when we were both single. Those evolved into painting what-if scenarios detailing our lives together had we met before I had married. We began exchanging song lyrics, poems and stories, all centered on our hypothetical relationship.

That next week, my family and I were headed out of town to visit extended family early for Christmas. When my new friend claimed he didn't know how he could make it a week without talking to me, I quickly gave him my personal contact information. During that weekend, we connected through email and texts. Everyone was already accustomed to me glued to the computer or phone, so it was nothing out of the ordinary to see me typing away at every chance I had.

That snowy weekend was a turning point. By the time I came home, I was playing out fantastical scenes with this guy in my mind. I made another epic error upon returning by telling him about these fantasies. As you could imagine, things escalated even more until it finally pinnacled to chatting one night until the wee hours of the morning about things that made my very married cheeks blush. After that night, I insisted conversations could not veer down such an intimate path again, yet we continued our relationship in all other ways. We still were trying to imagine life together. We still were hiding conversations. We still were anxious to see one another.

At work, we barely spoke to one another. We never were inappropriate in front of our coworkers. We never saw each other outside of work. Our colleagues knew we were good friends but I don't think anyone could guess what was developing.

Three weeks later, Christmas was approaching, and I found myself in a very precarious position. Each conversation seemed like a small jump from the last one but suddenly, somehow, I was knee-deep.

I was skirting the truth about what I was doing on the computer. I had to squash smiles in response to reading texts on my phone. I was thinking about him nonstop. I was writing poetry and short stories. I was barely eating and I'd lost several pounds from the anticipation of what was going to happen next with him and anxiety regarding what could happen if Scott found out. My thoughts were held captive by fantasies and what-if scenarios. I had become obsessed. And the feelings were very much returned.

We were very open about our emotions, about our surprise at how fast things had escalated and where things were going. We talked over and over about lines we had drawn and how we were constantly overstepping them. But I felt like there was nothing I couldn't say to him. I had gotten to the point where I felt as if I needed him in my life.

A simple question Scott asked a few days after Christmas left me no edge to skirt around. I simply could not produce an all-out lie when I was beginning to see just how deep a grave I had been digging for myself. Not to mention my family.

Confession

Theme Song:

Somewhere in the Middle, Casting Crowns

"Is there anything going on with this guy that I wouldn't like?" It was a vague question but would not be a vague answer. He could have asked if it was an affair and I would have easily justified that it was not. He could have asked if I was in love with him and clearly I was not. He could have asked if I wanted to leave the marriage and of course I did not. He could have asked if I wanted a divorce and clearly I did not. But was there anything going on with this guy that he wouldn't like? The answer was a big fat *yes*.

I answered his question with the truth. I could feel my heart race, my face flood and my eyes fill with tears as I explained that yes, there had been some *stuff* happening. I was quick to clarify nothing physical but *stuff* all the same. I'm not even sure I knew what this stuff entailed or had a name but I knew *stuff* had happened. I confessed to conversations he wouldn't have approved of but I didn't give away every single detail. It wasn't that I wanted it to remain private to me and this guy, it's just that I didn't want to hurt Scott any more than I already had. I felt like every detail was another dagger. The basic message I gave him through my tears was that I had been hiding conversations and some of them had been intimate.

We were in our bedroom. I sat on our bed and I watched as he slammed the closet door shut. His face scowled and the yelling began. *Of course.* I've blocked out much of what happened in that conversation.

I was so emotional I just remember him saying I should pack up and leave even though I knew he would never want that. He asked if I wanted to leave and I assured him I did not. No one could blame his angry response. I was virtually being intimate with another man. No, not physically, but yes, emotionally. What I love him for though was that he never mentioned a divorce. Ever. We may have been miserable but never was divorce an option.

But we were miserable, there's no doubt.

During that first conversation, I tried to negotiate my relationship with this guy. Why do I have to stop if it's just conversations? Aren't I allowed friends? My regret was mixed in with grief and anger. I remember being so confused at my feelings.

My loyalty to Scott was never a question. I'd been with him since I was 15 and I truly did not know life without him. I loved him and I loved our family. This new relationship was never meant to replace my current one. I somehow believed I could have both. Scott was amazing and he would assure me that he didn't mind him as a friend but the deception and intimate talks would have to stop.

To satisfy Scott's requirements and do what I truly knew to be best deep down, I told this man Scott had found out and I was making a decision to work on our marriage. Although the decision was never a difficult one, I needed to be clear with him that things were going to change. I asked that from then on, the conversations remain above-board and work-related.

Beyond being shamed and hurt for what I had done to Scott, another part of me was simply sad. Although I felt regret for the infidelity, I still felt a deep connection to this new person. When I would cry, which was often over the next few days, most of it was because I knew I'd be losing one of my closest confidantes. The easy conversations and laughter would be gone.

At this point you'd think it would be easy. A decision had been made. Cut and dry. Not exactly. I faltered more times than I can count. It was a near-physical effort not to say what I wanted to say to this person. At one point I changed my screen name on my instant messenger with an additional K.I.C. to remind myself to "keep it clean" during our required chat sessions. Replies that had become second-nature now had to be stifled. When something happened and I wanted to tell someone, no longer could I go to him. But even though I couldn't, I did. Many times. And each time I failed, I would tell Scott. He would always roll his eyes and give me the silent treatment in anger until I convinced him to talk it out with me and he forgave me. It took months for the relationship to return platonic. And even years later, I could feel myself wanting to slip into old habits with this man.

Along the way, God led me to share more and more details with Scott about those details I'd originally shielded. I felt as if I was still deceiving him about what had occurred. And to be honest, I was coming out of the haze. I would suddenly feel convicted over something that previously had not bothered me. The words, "I need to tell you something," became well-known and well-hated in our house. Scott knew another confession, whether it was a new transgression or an old un-confessed old one was coming. We always tease Scott that he has no patience, but during those years, he had more patience with me than I deserved.

It has taken years for my feelings to completely work themselves out, but they eventually did. As work requirements changed and it was no longer necessary to talk to him, life became much easier. Also, God was doing work necessary in myself and Scott individually that truly made the difference in our marriage.

SECTION II

THE THORNS

I've shared my story thus far. I look forward to sharing how God was working in my life during this process, as that's ultimately how I was rescued. However, I feel it's important for you to recognize whether you are traveling the same path. Section II deals with the practicalities of what these relationships look like so you know if you need to raise a flag to get out.

Signs

Theme Song:

Haunted, Taylor Swift

Just a month after this situation began, I started reading the Beth Moore study, When Godly People do Ungodly Things. The first week contained a list of 16 common claims of the seduced or, in other words, someone entangled in an emotional affair. While at some level, I knew I had been seduced before even reading the list, something about making all the checkmarks opened my eyes to the seriousness of my situation. Out of the 16, I checked the following:

- Individuals were caught off guard by a sudden onslaught of temptation or attack.
- The season of overwhelming temptation and seduction often followed huge spiritual markers with God.
- Everyone described a mental bombardment.
- Many of those caught in relational seductions testified that Satan got to them through someone close by.
- Many testified to early warning signals.
- Many described their sudden behavioral patterns as totally uncharacteristic.
- Virtually all of them described feelings and practices of isolation.
- Without exception, deception and some level of secrecy were involved.
- Many described something we'll call an addictive nature to the seductive sin.
- Most utterly hated what they were doing.
- The seduction lasted only for a season.
- Many describe the aftermath as a time of slowly increasing awareness rather than an instant wake up.

Yep, I checked all but 4 on the list. After reading that, my eyes were completely opened to the fact that I had become entangled. Perhaps you could identify with items on the list as well. I highly recommend Beth's study so you can go explore each of these points and find other truths.

Several years ago I began to feel as if God might want me to share about my entanglement. While I was not ready to fully write this manuscript, I knew I needed to write down what my emotional affair was like before too much time passed. Since it had only been a few years since it had happened, I could clearly remember characteristics of our relationship that were unlike any other friendship I had. Now that even more time has passed, I look back at some of things I did and am deeply humiliated. That person is not the person I am today. However, in the thick of the situation, it all seemed completely acceptable. I've taken all of those things I experienced and developed my own specialized list of practical actions and thoughts that characterized my emotional affair hoping that you might connect to them to see if you are indeed experiencing an emotional affair.

On their own, some of these actions are harmless, but if 2, 3 or more are characteristic of a relationship, I would suggest it is an emotional affair.

Your accelerated heart beat gives you away.

Physical evidence, such as a heartbeat, doesn't seem like much proof of anything but life. However, I submit that physical evidence of an emotional affair can exist. One example is the age-old saying "You make my heart race," which someone tells a person he or she is dating. You physically respond when you are complimented or when you are looking forward to seeing them. The anticipation and excitation of something new and interesting happening quickens your pulse. Whether we like to or admit or not, the beginnings of an emotional affair share many similarities found when dating someone new.

The second reason your heart might race is because of the level of anxiety involved in getting caught. The longer it goes on, the worse it gets. Once you are entrenched in the relationship and you realize what is happening has crossed a line, you have even more of a desire to cover up the infidelity.

Your lack of appetite is noticeable.

Physical evidence continues with a lack of appetite. Because of your high anxiety level, you might find that you can't settle down enough to eat. If you do eat, it doesn't sit well. You may even go as far as having ulcers or digestive issues.

You feel exhausted.

The final physical evidence I would suggest is being tired. Anxiety and stress are well-known to lead to sleep issues. When you should be sleeping, you are spending time daydreaming about what was talked about that day, what communication you're looking forward to the next day or even worrying what will happen if your spouse discovers your secret. In addition, you may find yourself tired because you are staying up late to flirt with this person. If your spouse works nights, you may be using his work time to communicate. Or, you may be getting out of bed after your spouse is asleep to talk to your new friend.

One night, in my parents' vacation home, I was barely programming a web site as I waited for an email response from this man. My heart was about to beat out of my chest because on one hand I was anxiously anticipating this email and on the other, my entire family sat *in the same room* as me and I just knew they all were going to find out somehow. Earlier that day I had barely eaten what was typically my favorite sub. When I finally got the email, my heart sped. Later that night I tossed and turned mulling over the email. It was one of those days that all these physical responses were screaming evidence of an emotional affair.

You think about him all the time.

"What percentage would you say you think about me?" he asked me one time.

"Ninety percent," I answered with little hesitation.

Ninety percent. That's how much I admitted thinking about this person. At some level, I had him on my mind. Either I saw something that reminded me of him, I did or said something I wanted to tell him about, I was mulling over something he had said, or I was daydreaming and fantasizing.

Your daydreams are consumed with him.

Your thought-life and daydreams are a huge part of an emotional affair. Depending on which level the emotional affair is on, they will appear differently from someone else's daydreams.

Typically in the beginning, you may find that when you imagine situations between you and this person, the settings and even activities include things that typically you would never do. You may daydream about a safari in Africa together, backpacking through Europe, or floating on the French Riveria. Things that in theory you likely haven't found yourself realistically planning. My daydreams were often set in the mountains regardless of the fact I'm a beach girl and always have been. My honeymoon was on the coast of Florida. Daydreaming about a snowy setting is uncharacteristic for me.

As the relationship progresses, content of the daydreams may change. The more you get to know this new person and his routine, the more you may consider what life would be like with him. Daydreams may become more realistic. Watching Sunday afternoon football together, going out to eat with his friends or attending his cousin's wedding now occupies your mind.

You wish you'd never met your husband or you fantasize about his death.

This is a hard one to admit. But at some point you may begin to believe that you have met your soul mate in this other person and you wonder *what if*. What if we'd met at a different time? What if we met before I met my spouse? What if my spouse were to pass away? The scenarios become part of the fantasy. Suddenly the storyline is a Nicholas Sparks book. You're faithfully married, meet your true soul mate but choose your husband. Your husband dies and eventually you and your soul mate are reunited and live happily ever after.

Or maybe you consider what would have happened had you somehow run into this other person just one day before your future husband. Since Scott and I met so young, I often wondered if I would have been better to have married later in life, giving us a chance to meet.

While it sounds grotesque and insensitive to say you think of your spouse's death, the point is you are fantasizing how to be both the faithful wife and be a part of this person's life.

Songs make you think of him. You may share lyrics.

A song comes on the radio and the lyrics fit perfectly for how you feel. Star-crossed lovers that have never been together. A couple that has just broken up and are longing for each other. You want to share the song with him. Perhaps you have it playing on your computer when he comes to visit you at your desk. Or maybe you have it playing when you and your coworkers take your car out to lunch. Maybe you even send the song and lyrics to say how you feel instead of coming out and saying them yourself. Or perhaps you have a playlist together of songs that make you think of each other.

Songs were a huge part of my emotional affair and we were constantly sharing lyrics back and forth. There are some songs I cannot listen to today because it brings back the memories.

You write poems or stories reflecting feelings or fantasies.

You may find yourself writing poetry, songs or stories. Or maybe you're on the receiving end. With so much emotional turmoil, it's bound to come out in some way. I've never been a poet or songwriter but found myself writing both. I share part of a short story I wrote in a later chapter.

You think of him when you dress or fix your hair.

I find that this is always one of the first clues that my feelings are veering in a direction they shouldn't. It's natural to want to look good for people but you may find that you start wearing a dress often that he specifically complimented. Or perhaps he's mentioned he likes women with long hair, so you start growing yours out. Your end goal: more attention, more compliments.

You confess dreams or feelings for each other.

You may find you're incredibly open with this person. He's the one you turn to when something new is happening. You want his advice on your problems. When you've accomplished something, you want his praise. You even confess about your turmoil over him *to him*. You tell him how you felt the last time you saw him. You talk about how you miss him. You talk about how wrong your feelings are. You talk about how right your feelings are. We often said we were like two 14-year-old girls that talk about everything. We could have talked for hours. And hours.

You find reasons to give gifts.

Birthdays, Christmases, Valentine's Days are all good reasons to buy your romantic interest a gift. You want to buy him gifts all the time to show how you feel, and you may find these holidays are perfect excuses. You might even find yourself buying *other* people gifts just so your gift to this person doesn't look odd.

For example, you may have discussed baking chocolate chip cookies for him on a cold winter day. In order to actually play this out in real life, you'll make everyone in the office chocolate chip cookies and then make sure he knows you made them and offer him some. In all honesty you both know they were for him. I never gave him gifts but often thought of ways I could have.

You desire to see him or being where you know he will be.

You may find yourself inordinately anxious to see this person. You may see him at the movies and yes, it's exciting to go to the movies but do you typically get that excited over running into other friends? Maybe you see this person at the gym. You know if you're excited about going to the sweat-fest you typically dread, there is something wrong!

Since this man was at my work, I found myself looking forward to getting to work when that certainly had never been the case before.

Find reasons to see each other.

Because you desire to see them in regular settings, you find other ways to see him more frequently. If you work with this person, you may find yourself planning extra meetings. If you met him at the gym, suddenly you are going 7 days a week. You might suddenly become Sunday School Suzie with all the time you begin spending at your church. You will search for any logical reason to create another environment where you can be together.

At the time, I worked from home without a normal schedule to be in the office but I often found myself wanting to plan extra days in the office so I could see him.

You allow yourself to be alone with him.

You may not normally allow yourself to go to lunch, dinner or coffee alone with someone but for this person, you make an exception. We often went to lunch on our own although I never did the same with any other male coworker.

When you're not together you remain connected. Your spouse is unaware.

Usually contact happens in a form other than face to face. As time goes by, the number of ways you contact one another increases. For me, it all started with work email. Then personal email. And then we added each other on social networking. Suddenly we were texting constantly. We were trying to find every way we could to keep in contact. And most, if not all of that, was hidden from my husband. Emails were deleted as soon as they were read. Files holding the poems and stories were archived and hidden in my file system on my computer. His name was obscured on my phone so it was not obvious who is calling or texting. While I didn't, others go so far as to hide Facebook or Twitter passwords or even create separate accounts on these sites to hide conversations.

Friends and family remain clueless.

Because you are talking to this person so much, he is bound to slip into conversation with family and friends. Oh, Jason at the gym or Bob at work or Carl I went to school with. They'll know who he is and you may even update them with updates about him. But they have no idea the types of conversations you've had. If they were to find out, you'd be mortified.

Both my husband and sister knew I texted this man on a regular basis but thought we were just friends. Neither had any idea the extent of the relationship.

You refer to each other as girlfriend/boyfriend or office wife/husband.

This is a common office practice these days. A lot of times a guy and girl that spend a lot of time together at the office are given nicknames from coworkers. Bob? Oh yes, he's Ann's office boyfriend. Usually if someone wants to find out where Ann is, they talk to Bob. If Bob wants coffee, Ann will go. If Ann needs to run an errand, Bob will tag along. If there is an office dispute, they are "going to break up".

Everyone knew we were good friends and anytime someone had a question about either of us, our colleagues always asked the other. As I mentioned, we often went to lunch together and when we were in group settings, they knew we wanted to sit together.

When you are entangled in these relationships, it's very difficult to discern acceptable behavior and thoughts. The conversations or actions seem innocent individually. When my mind tried to justify what I was actually doing, it never seemed like a big deal. "So, we talked about a song today. So what?" was a typical thought. However, when you begin to pair these actions together, it becomes clear the relationship is inappropriate.

If you find yourself relating to more than a couple of these, even seemingly innocent signs, I would say it's likely you are beginning or fully involved in an emotional affair. I'm no expert. I didn't take a poll. I haven't interviewed hundreds of people. It is simply what I experienced.

For those that are not relating to the list, use these as warning signs rather than a diagnosis. Perhaps you could stop a relationship before escalates if you can recognize early signs. Clearly, you won't be writing poems about a platonic coworker but you may find that you have started caring about his opinion more often than before or caring about how you dress around him. Even after what I went through, I can feel myself slipping into some of these habits with a new person. One of the first signs I've always seen in myself is caring about how I look for a person. If I'm suddenly caring about what a particular man thinks of how I am dressed, I know now it is a red flag. I'm now able to immediately recognize that pattern and guard against my emotions getting out of control.

An Emotional Affair

In the last chapter we dealt with the signs of an emotional affair. Perhaps while reading you nodded your head in agreement the entire time. Maybe you checked off more checkmarks than you'd like to admit. Or perhaps you only recognized one or two and you're doubtful this whole "emotional affair" thing is applicable to you. Know this: affairs (emotional or otherwise) don't happen overnight. While they can happen more quickly than I'd like to admit, there usually is a progression of feelings and actions.

So let's go back to high school for a moment, back to a quite tangible measure for relationships: the baseball analogy. First base was kissing, second, third, until fourth was "all the way". You could tell how far the relationship had progressed by how many bases were run. I remember, even as late as college, asking my friend if she had "played baseball" on her date the night before. Sometimes people rounded those bases really fast but slow or fast, every base was visited.

Emotional affairs are a lot more complicated than grade-school games with crushes, but there is a similar pattern of progression on an emotional level. All emotional affairs are going to progress at different speeds. Some people will be friends with a person for a long time before ever considering running to first base and then they're to third before they know it. Other people pause to rest between each base. The same thing happens on an emotional level. Some people attach themselves to people very quickly and sail right through the emotional bases while others take it slowly.

Here are four stages in which these emotional affairs travel.

Four stages

Stage 1

If your emotional affair is in the beginning stages, you may have only related to one or two of the signs in the previous chapter. At this stage, you might find yourself simply thinking about him more than you think about your average friend. You wonder about what he thinks of your outfit. You might speculate about what he's doing when you're not together. You always look forward to seeing him again. Also, you get along really well together. The relationship feels fairly innocent at this point. However, when compared to relationships with others of a similar nature, there is something a little different about this one.

Stage 2

In Stage 2, you begin to wonder *what if.* At this level you begin to fantasize what it may be like to be with him romantically. You might even begin discussions with him about fantasy dream dates. It doesn't have to mean you've gone to the physical realm with this person even in your head. But you start to see him as your fairy-tale costar. If you're Cinderella, he's Prince Charming. You attend a ball together and lose your slipper and he chases after you through all the land. Perhaps when you read a novel, you imagine him as the lead character. When you hear love songs, he's the one you're thinking about. At this stage, a lot of internal fantasizing is going on.

Stage 3

In Stage 3, things are getting really serious. You're having conversations with him that you've never had with anyone. Maybe not even your husband or a serious boyfriend. No longer are you just thinking about your feelings, but now you're discussing them with him. You're longing to be with him constantly. You are starting to get to know him on a personal level, so you have a lot more daily topics. You can't wait to tell him what happened the night before. You can't wait to hear about his night. At this stage, you might start feeling that accelerated heartbeat when you see him. If your conversations were monitored, you'd be mortified. You are texting or messaging constantly even though that hasn't been the case before. Things are getting intense. Emotional affairs rarely end here. You will reach Stage 4 in no time at all.

Stage 4

During Stage 4, all of the above is happening but at an even more intense level. At this point, this man is a very tangible fixture in your life. The two of you know each other's personal struggles and daily rituals. It's at this stage you start to wonder if your husband is really your soul mate. You may begin to fantasize scenarios where you lose your husband or divorce him. You wonder what it would be like to be this new man's wife. You imagine yourself in their daily rituals with him. If you're creative, you're probably writing poems, stories or songs to each other. Songs on the radio constantly remind you of him. You discuss the future with him and consider if the two of you would ever work as a real-life couple. You can't seem to see each other enough and arrange extra time to be together, alone even. This relationship is completely locked down and hidden from your spouse and your anxiety level is at a maximum. You can't quit thinking about him and you may even admit to yourself this person is like an addiction or obsession.

At Stage 4, we are looking at a full-blown emotional affair. This type of relationship rarely fizzles but only intensifies until it is discovered or is stopped by one of the parties.

In my case, we traveled at warp speed. One day we were friends and within weeks we were well into Stage 4. The scary thing about Stage 4 is once you are done with that inning, you usually want to play again. But the next inning will be different. You start this thing out saying you could never cheat on your husband but when emotions are running high in Stage 4, it's a natural instinct to want to act on your feelings, even while convincing yourself you don't want to or never would actually have a *real affair*. Trust me, you don't want to play that game. That's why it's so important to recognize where you are and stop it from progressing any further.

It's just …

If you're at any of these stages, you probably would have said you wouldn't have believed you'd be capable of going to any of these stages … ever. I have found there is a key phrase that gets you to the next stage without you ever even realizing what's happening. And that is: "it's just …".

We say this all the time to rationalize all kinds of things. If you're on a diet and you want dessert, you say, "It's just one piece of cake." If you're on an exercise plan and you don't feel like going one day, you say, "It's just one day, I can get back on track tomorrow." If you're out with friends, you might say, "It's just one drink." You see the picture. Rarely is it just anything. Those small things turn into habits and before you know it, you've blown any resolve you had at the start.

With an emotional affair, it always starts with something like "it's just lunch with a friend." In Stage 2, "it's just a daydream; I'm allowed to daydream." In Stage 3, "he's just a good friend; I really need one." In Stage 4, "It's just a poem." "It's just a song." "It's just a conversation." "It's just lunch." "It's just a text message."

The point is, you don't wake up one day into Stage 4 from nothing. The progression is often paved with excuses or justifications. The problem is each base seems impossible to get to until you look up and realize you've slid into the next base without any issue at all.

Emotions

In an emotional affair, one experiences a lot of, well, emotions. I've never experienced so many different feelings in such a short amount of time as I did during the progression, confession and healing of my emotional affair. I want to name some of those emotions. Naming these emotions will help you recognize what you're feeling is normal, but know that if you're feeling them, it's another red flag that you're in an emotional affair.

• Anger

If you aren't angry before this happens, you might start feeling angry. You start to become angry at your husband for not treating you the way you feel like you deserve. You are angry at yourself for not making decisions earlier in life that could have put you with this new man. You are angry with yourself for continuing in the infidelity. And you just might be angry at God for allowing any of it to happen.

• Loneliness

Loneliness seems an odd description, as you and this man are having intimate conversations. But hear me out: you can't tell anyone. You feel guilty even praying about it. Eventually, you begin to feel alone in this fight.

· Excitement

Emotional affairs can be an exciting time. You have feelings you haven't felt in a long time, if ever. If your marriage is not something you want to continue and you're making future plans with this person, it could be exciting to think you finally have a relationship that's going to work out.

· Guilt

The guilt is overriding. Although you like this person and how they make you feel, something deep down (or not so deep down) knows that it's all kinds of wrong. While you are thoroughly enjoying yourself, you know your actions would devastate your spouse and the rest of your family.

· Love

You might be feeling more loved than you have felt in a long time. For once, someone is spending time with you, actually listening to you, wanting to do things for you.

· Hope

Perhaps you have long since given up on your marriage. Everything felt doomed before. You'd never feel loved or desired again. This person has reminded you that you are still attractive, wanted and desired and there is hope in this new relationship.

· Adoration

You are certain you've never felt quite so special. There seems to be something special about the way he feels about you and you don't want the feeling to go away.

• Regret

You probably aren't quite yet regretting your actions in the emotional affair but you might regret getting married. Maybe this person is an old boyfriend and you regret ever letting him go. Maybe you regret waiting just a few years to get married — that way, would have met this guy. If you're in Stage 4, you are feeling as if you're in over your head. You regret that you ever got yourself into this mess but that is likely over run by the adoration, hope and excitement.

• Shame

When a serious relationship and intense feelings are written and pointed out, maybe for this first time, you might start feeling very shameful of the relationship and your choices. It's all completely normal. No, it's not good that you're in this relationship but it's good that you are recognizing and naming what is going on.

You're not alone. I know all of these feelings. It's normal to be feeling all of them in varying degrees all at the same time.

The heart of the problem

So, we have talked a lot of details about emotional affairs: signs, stages and emotions. But I want to talk about an indicator that supersedes all of these: your desire to please this person. At all stages, what sets this person apart from other in your life is that you care deeply about what he thinks. Whether it's your outfit in Stage 1 or your kids in Stage 4, your main motive is to please this person so he will in turn please you. I was in such a vicious cycle with this person at times. He fed my ego, I fed his and we would talk nonstop until we were on this emotional high that made us feel like giddy teenagers. It's quite addictive. But it means you've given your heart away to a man that is not your husband.

You may buck at that and say *my real feelings are not involved*. But your actions belie your words.

When we became Christians, an amazing thing happened. We started caring a whole lot about what God thought of us. And it wasn't just that we wanted to stay on the straight and narrow out of fear. There is something in us that really wants to please Him. I have never talked to one Christian who admitted that they really weren't looking forward to hearing, "Well done, my good and faithful child." Because we love Him, we want to please Him. In most Christian circles, that time when we started caring is referred to the time we asked Him in our hearts, or when we gave Him our hearts. It is quite simply the time we began our faith journey. The decision to trust in God comes from within.

If you look back, you'll realize you recognize these emotions. Remember when you started dating your spouse? You would have done just about anything to win his affection. You would dine at his favorite restaurant. You would dress in a way you knew he found attractive. You attended sporting events that you wouldn't normally go to. You watched movies that you never considered watching. It's because he had won your heart or you gave him your heart. There is a symbol for this — remember the unity candle? Your hearts are not two, but one. The physical aspect is then consummated on the wedding night.

In an emotional affair, you do not give ourselves physically to a person. In a physical affair, your body is given to a person that is not your spouse, breaking all the bonds that are sacred in marriage. But in an emotional affair, there are still bonds that are broken. You don't give your body, sure, but you do give your heart to a person that is not your spouse. Your behavior shows you have given your heart away. This emotional bond is every bit of important and sacred as the physical.

Whether you'd like to admit it, you have created an emotional bond to this person. That's why it's so hard to walk away. I remember thinking of every way I could to rationalize its impact away and to stay in the infidelity. I truly understand what you are feeling. Don't worry, we'll deal with that.

Living in lala land

Before we examine why and how we rationalize these relationships, I want to talk more about this emotional bond. Particularly in Stage 4, you may feel as if the connection is so strong that it must mean you have found true love. Since you are no longer feeling a spark with your spouse, it must mean that you made a mistake marrying him and these new feelings indicate who your true soul mate is.

While I will not deny there are strong bonds, I want to be clear that they are not true love. What I found so profoundly interesting about this relationship, and I am not the only one to testify to this, is the new person is not someone I could be with long term. When prompted in a discussion with a friend about emotional affairs, I rattled off at least 5 good reasons I could not ever be with him long term. For instance, our religious differences I mentioned earlier would be enough to be a deal-breaker. And while I never really had planned to leave my husband and marry him, I certainly at the time felt as if I couldn't live without the feeling I had with the new guy.

I love what Pastor Andy Stanley said in his sermon series Love, Sex & Dating. He says you can experience passion with just about anyone. That feeling we're having is not love. Love is an enduring, truthful, pure choice we make with our spouses, acknowledging and accepting all of each other's faults. That feeling you seek is what fairy tales are made of. If you left your husband, you might have a wonderful few days, weeks or even months enjoying the chemistry with this new guy, but when that wears off, what will be left? In my case, I would have been devastated. And you may feel like you're giving up a fairy tale by giving up this person but listen up: You didn't lose a fairy tale with your husband and you aren't giving up a fairy tale by giving up this person. Because guess what? Fairy tales don't exist. There is not one couple whose relationship is like a fairy tale. Ever. In the history of relationships. That feeling is what is known as the affair fog. Reality has been suspended. During this time, all the person's faults are discarded and all you see and believe in is the good stuff in lala land. Chemistry, on its own, is always temporary. That's not to say you won't have bouts of recharged chemistry throughout a relationship but that is not what sustains it. Lasting relationships and love are hard work. You have to fight to make love last for 40, 50 and 60 years.

The only thing you give up when you exit the affair is a false sense of hope. But what you keep is a legacy with your spouse. You have a choice on how your story is written. What I envision at the end of my marriage is what I know of a sweet couple in their 90s. They've known each other since they were 5 and have been married over 70 years. That love? It's not fake. That's a love that endured. That forgave. That was faithful. That was pure. We will never have that kind of story if we don't give up the false and temporary.

And yet? I know what you are feeling. Logically, you understand everything I just told you. Yet, you still want to hold on. Let's tear apart all of your excuses, why don't we?

Justifications

Theme Song:

Need You Now, Lady Antebellum

After my husband found out what was going on, I was heartbroken. I was ashamed at how bad things had gotten and remorseful, but at the same time I was fighting to reason out ways to continue this friendship. I couldn't imagine going through my day without my new friend. There are some justifications I tried to use to keep it going. See if you can relate to any of these.

It's just pretend.

One of the signs we talked about was that your daydreams can be fantastical or grandiose. You're not dreaming of anything as serious as having his children, just what a fun vacation together might be like. Because most of your thoughts are unrealistic, you tell yourself it's doing no one any harm. Even if the fantasies are realistic, they are just daydreams. It's just thoughts, right? A person is allowed to dream.

This would never happen in real life.

Again, because the daydreams are unrealistic, you tell yourself it's not possible at all for it to happen in real life. Neither of you have the money to get to France, pay for a hotel and then ride down the Riveria. So there is no logistical way for it to happen. So why worry about it? More than that though, you may find yourself with someone that you would never actually date in real life. Maybe, like me, you have a different religious background or a habit you couldn't live with or maybe they are not physically appealing to you. No matter the reason, you don't believe being with this person could happen realistically.

As long as it isn't physical, it's ok.

Real affairs happen when physical stuff happens. As long as I'm being physically faithful, what's the harm? When it comes right down to it, we're just talking. No big deal.

You talk about faith. You believe you're helping him. Or, he's helping you.

You may find that your initial connection with this person is spiritual. Perhaps you met at church and the reason you started talking more was because you agreed on so many things or you really just enjoyed conversing with them. Or your different religious backgrounds allow for the ability to discuss and debate in a healthy manner. In any case, you believe it's benefiting one or both of you to continue talking.

It helps your marriage.

Because you are being fed emotionally, you may actually be responding to your husband's advances better. Perhaps you are using physical desires of this person to fuel thoughts in the bedroom you share with your husband.

Or, maybe you've realized your husband doesn't treat you well and you actually speak to him about it. He responds by working harder to please you. You believe it's all a fantastic result of the emotional affair.

You would never cheat on your husband.

Even if you are aware the conversations are out of bounds, you believe you could never physically cheat on your husband. No harm done.

You don't even see each other physically.

In many cases you may have never met this person physically or rarely see him. In some cases, it may have been years since you've seen him. Perhaps you talk online or through texts. Since there is no chance of a physical affair, it's not an issue.

He's your soul mate. If only you'd met at a different time.

You may justify your behavior because you believe that this is your soul mate. He was the one you were supposed to be with to begin with and you should be together. You tell yourself, "I'm going to continue talking with him because I need him. He's my soul mate, after all."

He's better than your husband.

You may feel that your husband treats you poorly, but this guy knows how you are supposed to be treated. You feel like a queen when you talk to him and if your husband won't treat me like that, someone ought to.

Your husband doesn't deserve your attention anyway.

You may feel ready to move on, at least emotionally if not physically. Your heart is already gone from that relationship and your husband doesn't deserve your attention.

Your husband deserves your betrayal.

Your husband not only doesn't deserve your attention but maybe he deserves one step further … betrayal. Maybe your husband has already had an affair. While you can't bring yourself to physically cheat, you are getting him back by emotionally stepping out.

You're really just friends. You don't know what you'd do without him.

Because you tell the new man everything that is going on, you may feel as if you lose your connection to him, your life will fall apart. You have no one else to turn to and he keeps you sane. He's your friend. A person is allowed friends.

Your husband knows about him. If he had a problem, he'd tell you.

Maybe your husband is familiar with your relationship with the guy. Maybe he sees the flirting or explicit emails but he doesn't say anything to you. You're fine with it as long as he is.

You have enough love for both. They both meet different needs.

You believe you can have both men in your life. Your husband meets your physical needs and he meets your emotional needs. Or perhaps your husband is a pretty good guy and this other one is too. No matter, you have enough love in your heart for both of them. It's a little like having another child: your heart just expands and you can manage both. Each serve their own purpose and you love them both in different ways.

These are just the ways I convinced myself. It's your job to pinpoint your own excuses. Imagine this scenario: your best friend finds out about the relationship. She asks you to stop what you're doing but you say no and then list your reasons why. "I would stop but … " "I will when my husband stops … " "I deserve it because … " Those are your justifications. Depending on your circumstances, they may look different than mine. It's important to recognize why you are doing this.

A Choice

Theme Song:

Before the Morning, Josh Wilson

When Christian author and speaker Beth Moore holds her Living Proof Live conferences she does not have a predetermined set of talks to give. Before each conference weekend, she asks God for a word. She jokes that God takes her literally and she usually gets just a word. When I attended her Charlotte event, we were lucky and got two words "Hold Fast".

If I have one word for this whole book, here it is:

STOP.

If you have found yourself relating to the last few chapters, *stop* is your word. As acceptable and even good the relationship might seem to you right now, it needs to stop. This is decision time and I need to be frank and direct. If you continue the path you've been on, things are only going to escalate into a physical affair. If you want to save your marriage and family, you must choose to end this relationship.

Over and over, God calls us to obedience. You can't wait until you feel like obeying. You can't wait until you are ready to give this person up. I am telling you, your family will have packed up their things and moved on before that day will come. You won't want to end this, you won't feel like stopping it, you won't understand why you're ending it. But you have to stop this. You are responsible.

Not when the other man says it's enough.

Not when your husband says it's enough.

Not when the other man says you've crossed another line.

Not when your husband finds out.

Not when your mother asks what you're doing.

Not when your sister calls you out.

Not tomorrow.

Not six months from now.

Not a year from now.

Whether you've been caught or you've just realized you're in an emotional affair. The bottom line is:

You
must
stop.

You. And only you have the power to control this. You feel you are the only one that understands what you feel for this person and what you've done. You have put yourself in this situation and only you can get yourself out.

Put a stop to it with the person. Especially if you are the one who is married. You are the one with all the stakes. This other person has nothing to gain but a beautiful, smart woman and possibly a built-in family.

You have to go to him, in a letter, email, on the phone or in person. You have to explain that a choice must be made and you are choosing your husband. This man is not welcome to play house with you anymore. He shouldn't text, email, call, Facebook, tweet, visit, stalk or otherwise contact you.

After you talk to him you are to delete pictures, emails, texts, poems, stories, tweets and get rid of any gifts. You must remove any reminder of him. When you see these things, they are only keys to your memories that will ignite fires where embers remain. Change your phone number and your email if you need to. Quit your job if you must. Move to another city with your family if push comes to shove.

Your family is at stake. Do what it takes.

I failed in this. It took years for me to truly crawl out of the web I had woven. I am telling you from personal experience. Do not put yourself through years of this. Cut it off at the roots. It will hurt. Even with my quasi-"break-up", I cried and mourned, and at times I doubled over from all the hurt. I was shamed, yes, but most of me just hurt that I was losing the one person I felt I could say anything to. I understand a clean cut is going to feel like the knife went straight through your gut. But it must be done. I will give you hope and say you will come through. Over time you will feel that regret I mentioned, and your feelings will eventually catch up with your obedience. As my friend Dani often reminds me, until then you're going to have to fake it until you make it.

It will take a long time until you don't want to contact this person. In fact, it may be a lifelong struggle. But if you are truly committed to your marriage and family, you must take the steps even if your emotions are pulling you toward him.

I often have this conversation with my girls after I tell them to clean their room. They say, "But I don't feeelll like it!"

My immediate response is usually, "It doesn't matter how you feel, you just need to do it." We learn as we mature that sometimes we have to go through painful situations when we know that the end result is worth it. We clean our homes so we don't have ants from hidden food rotting somewhere. We do laundry so we aren't continually buying new clothes to wear. These chores we do are for our own good and we know that. This time of repentance and change will be painful. But it's your only way to save your family and reclaim your joy.

At this moment, some of you reading may be ready to give up your marriage and family for one reason or another. Whether you know this yet or not, the reason you are reading is because you do want help and want to salvage your marriage and family. Otherwise, you would not have bought this book. However, I want to be sensitive to the fact that you may truly have a horrible spouse. In fact, it is possible what drove you to this infidelity. For that I am very sorry. I want to encourage you, though, to take one step at a time. I can guarantee that your judgment about your marriage is severely clouded by this relationship. You cannot wisely, clearly, certainly make a choice when there is a third party involved. If nothing else, make the choice to end this affair so you can make a choice about your marriage. Do not let a false, deceitful, hypothetical relationship be the end to a true, albeit difficult marriage.

I debated putting a section in here dealing with how to handle your relationship if you are not able to stop talking to this person. Some people are stuck in a position where you just have to be around this person. But truly, there is no good way to stay in contact and end this all at the same time. If you can stop contact completely, that is the only way to stop any progression.

Even after I communicated to the guy things had to stop, I'll admit things probably got worse before they got better. So I do have this piece of advice to give: You're going to have be mature enough and strong enough to say no. And say no a lot. You have to say no to your thoughts. You have to say no to your mouth. You have to say no to this person. A lot. You have to learn the phrase, "This is not appropriate." You can make all the rules you want — and I do recommend making them — but you will fail. And when you do, you have to get back up, put your stake in the ground one more time and *stop*.

SECTION III

THE UNTANGLING

Stopping seems impossible at this moment. While the relationship may end abruptly, healing emotionally and spiritually will be a process. The following section is devoted to the spiritual healing and lessons I learned while fighting my way out of the maze. Maybe I can save you from learning the hard way and open your eyes to the work God is doing. I stopped my emotional affair out of obedience for God and respect for my marriage. The lessons I learned will keep me from walking these dead-end paths ever again.

Faith

Theme Song:

East to West, Casting Crowns

You might still be saying to yourself, *well what's the big deal?* It's certainly a question I asked myself. I didn't out and out lie to anyone. I didn't sleep with anyone. What really was the harm? It might seem obvious after the fact, or to someone who hasn't gone through this, but when you're in the thick of it, at times your actions just don't seem so bad. I can remember so many times telling Scott, "We're just friends." How is that sinful?

I would submit that the easiest sin to see is the lying and deception. Clearly, if you are lying to cover up actions you've taken, you have sinned. Furthermore, if you are going out of your way to conceal actions but not necessarily speaking straight-out lies, that is deception. And boy, did I take part in that. We will talk more about deceit in a later chapter.

I would also submit that the relationship was a sin against your husband and your marriage. Don't believe me? Ask your husband; I bet he will agree with me. Even still, let's take a closer look at why this is unacceptable.

During the Living Proof Live event I attended with Beth Moore recently, I mentioned that our theme words for the day were "hold fast". She did a word study that I'd like to share that I think will help you understand why the relationship itself is a sin.

In Job 41:15-17, the verse is describing the scales on a crocodile. It states:

His back has rows of shields
    tightly sealed together;
each is so close to the next
    that no air can pass between.
They are joined fast to one another;
    they cling together and cannot be parted.

That phrase "joined fast" is from the Hebrew word dabaq. It describes the picture of two things being held closely together. You can picture a crocodile's scales that are held so close together that no air can pass between them. In Job 19, Job continues that he's been so upset *"My bone cleaveth to my skin and to my flesh."* (KJV) That cleaveth is the same dabaq. Think of a sickly person when they are nothing but skin and bones. They are held fast together, with no fat to separate it. So now that we have this picture of things being joined fast "dabaq", let's see how Scripture uses that relating to marriage. In Genesis 2:24, the writer uses dabaq related to marriage. "Therefore shall a man leave his father and his mother, and shall cleave unto his wife: and they shall be one flesh." (KJV) The "cleave" is the same dabaq word. The man and wife are held fast together, with no air able to pass between them, as if they are glued together, much like scales on a crocodile or skin and bones. There should be nothing separating them. No deception, no secrets and certainly no person coming between them.

The word cleave is used 30 times in Scripture. The only other thing we should be cleaving to is God. Marriage is truly a three-part deal; husband and wife cleaving to one another, with each of them holding fast to God. There should be no air between any of them.

These emotional relationships take away from both your husband and God. You begin to look to this person to meet emotional needs he is not meant to satisfy. It's as if you are ungluing a part of yourself from your marriage and trying to attach it to another person.

Finally, for many of us, the simple fact is we have committed the sin of adultery. You may say *well, I never touched him, how can that be?* The Ten Commandments instructs us not to commit adultery. Some argue the Ten Commandments were something of the past from the Old Testament and not applicable to present-day Christians. However, if you study Jesus' words about the Ten Commandments, Jesus not only endorsed the Ten Commandments, but he also made them even more difficult to adhere to. Jesus himself says in Matthew 5:27-28 "'You have heard that it was said, 'Do not commit adultery.' But I tell you that anyone who looks at a woman lustfully has already committed adultery with her in his heart." I love what my Life Application Study Bible states in the commentary for verse 28: "To be faithful to your spouse with your body but not your mind is to break the trust so vital to a strong marriage. Jesus is not condemning natural interest in the opposite sex or even healthy sexual desire, but the deliberate and repeated filling of one's mind with fantasies that would be evil if acted out."

Now I will be the first to tell you that I don't believe women lust in the same way a man does. But if your emotional affair has gone on for any length of time, I cannot imagine that lust for this person did not play a part. And the simple truth that is hard to face is that this is adultery.

What I love about God is even when we can't see our sin for what it is, God doesn't leave us in it. He is so faithful to always call us back to Him. If you are His child, He will not let you continue in your sin. Many of you will have felt the Holy Spirit's conviction through this time, even unsure what it is you are doing wrong. That's Him saying, "No. I know this feels good in this moment, but it's not okay."

Before Christ was born, prophets pointed people to their sin. Jeremiah 35:15 states, "Again and again I sent all my servants, the prophets, to you. They said, 'Each of you must turn from your wicked ways and reform your actions...' But you have not paid attention or listened to me."

Since Christ resurrected and Pentecost occurred, we now have the Holy Spirit to convict us. Jesus says in John 16:7-8, "But I tell you the truth: It is for your good that I [Jesus] am going away. Unless I go away, the Counselor will not come to you; but if I go, I will send him to you. When he comes, he will convict the world of guilt in regard to sin and righteousness and judgment." God was faithful to us that not only did he send Jesus to save us from our sin, he left the Holy Spirit with us to continually convict us of our sin. He has the power to simply leave us in our sin. He has in the past simply wiped those not of him from the earth when he could no longer stand their sin. Think Noah or Sodom and Gomorrah. But he wants better for us than to stay in this sin and will woo us back to Him.

Conviction is like a rescue rope thrown from a boat. It's His way of saying come back, child, you are drowning in your sin, but I need to save you from yourself. When we feel that conviction, there is a decision to make. Will we continue in our strongholds or will we heed his direction? Proverbs 5:21-23 states

For a man's ways are in full view of the LORD,
    and he examines all his paths.
The evil deeds of a wicked man ensnare him;
    the cords of his sin hold him fast.
He will die for lack of discipline,
    led astray by his own great folly.

Will we grab on to his rope of salvation or will we "die for lack of discipline"? If we choose to grab on to the rope and be rescued, the practical tools by which we do that is confession and repentance. It is our way of demonstrating faithfulness back to him. To say *yes, I know your ways are good and right and even if I don't feel like it, I will follow you. I still believe in you, I have faith in you. I choose you.*

But again, God is so faithful, he doesn't ever, ever leave us alone when we confess. 1 John 1:9 states, "If we confess our sins, he is faithful and just and will forgive us our sins and purify us from all unrighteousness." In His faithfulness he accepts our confession and forgives us. We are the lost children, coming back to the boat. He greets us with a welcoming hug. We are back to life and no longer in danger of death.

Proverbs 28:13 states, "Whoever conceals their sins does not prosper, but the one who confesses *and renounces* them finds mercy." Your rescue is not complete, though, with only a confession. Yes, confession is necessary, but you must also renounce the sin you committed. Repentance, which means a turning away from your sin, must also occur. I found that I made the initial decision when I confessed to Scott that I would work on our marriage and that the infidelity needed to end. At that point, repentance began to take on flesh. Conversations between myself and this new guy were no longer. My thought processes were changed. My behavior began changing. That is repentance. Not only do we feel sorry and admit our transgressions, but we also make the necessary changes to stop it from happening again.

Your repentance, like mine, will most likely be a process. Although I intended my initial resolve to end this relationship, there were many times after I faltered. I confessed new transgressions to both God and Scott as they occurred. Confession and repentance was not a one-time deal. As we stumble in our path, we have to continually brush ourselves off and start again. There is no limit to God's forgiveness. The important thing, though, is that we do stand back up. If a conversation happens that shouldn't, circle back around and reset the ground rules. If you are listening to a song and thinking about this person, turn it off. If you are tempted to text the person, contact your husband or friend instead. You now know these individual things are not small grievances, but enormous pitfalls. Refuse to be entangled by them again.

During repentance, expect to experience sorrow. I found even though I had confessed to my husband and God, and my actions had turned in the other direction, I was still very grieved. I identified with David's psalms more than ever before. David was guilty of adultery and then murder to cover it, and it was clear he experienced regret and sorrow after this time. I still have many parts of Psalms underlined in my Bible from where my heart cried out to Him in the words of David many years ago:

For I know my transgressions,
    and my sin is always before me.
Against you, you only, have I sinned
    and done what is evil in your sight;
so you are right in your verdict
    and justified when you judge.
Surely I was sinful at birth,
    sinful from the time my mother conceived me.
Yet you desired faithfulness even in the womb;
    you taught me wisdom in that secret place.
Psalm 51:3-6

My guilt has overwhelmed me
    like a burden too heavy to bear.
 My wounds fester and are loathsome
    because of my sinful folly.
I am bowed down and brought very low;
    all day long I go about mourning.
My back is filled with searing pain;
    there is no health in my body.
I am feeble and utterly crushed;
    I groan in anguish of heart.

All my longings lie open before you, Lord;
    my sighing is not hidden from you.
My heart pounds, my strength fails me;
    even the light has gone from my eyes.

For I am about to fall,
    and my pain is ever with me.
I confess my iniquity;
    I am troubled by my sin.

LORD, do not forsake me;
    do not be far from me, my God.
Come quickly to help me,
    my Lord and my Savior.
Psalm 38:4-22

     All of those painful feelings still come rushing back to me as I read
through them. My spirit felt crushed that I had fallen so far. But God says
pour your heart out to Him. We don't need a best friend or counselor or
even a man to whom we need to pour out our feelings. God says in Psalm 62:

Find rest, O my soul, in God alone;
    my hope comes from him.
He alone is my rock and my salvation;
    he is my fortress, I will not be shaken.
My salvation and my honor depend on God;

he is my mighty rock, my refuge.
Trust in him at all times, O people;
    pour out your hearts to him,
    for God is our refuge.

Psalm 62:5-8

He is your rock. He is your refuge. Trust in Him. Pour your heart out to Him. I imagine there is no better cry to God than the cry of a beloved child sorrowful in his sin and wanting to make things right. The whole reason He won't let you go is because He wants to commune with you. Don't feel like you have to fix your problems before you go to God. He wants you to come to Him *with* your problems.

But joy, it does cometh. James 4:7-10 states:

Submit yourselves, then, to God. Resist the devil, and he will flee from you. Come near to God and he will come near to you. Wash your hands, you sinners, and purify your hearts, you double-minded. Grieve, mourn and wail. Change your laughter to mourning and your joy to gloom. Humble yourselves before the Lord, and he will lift you up.

He says, yes, grieve, mourn and wail but when you do it unto Me, I will lift you up. He turns our mourning into joy and we are lifted up. John 15:10-11 is another promise that joy comes when we begin to obey.

If you obey my commands, you will remain in my love, just as I have obeyed my Father's commands and remain in his love. I have told you this so that my joy may be in you and that your joy may be complete.

Our joy will be complete. I don't know about you but when I was in this time of mourning I sure needed some joy. My heart felt so dry. I was desperate for love and comfort. His path is the way. He convicts, we confess, He forgives and our joy is made complete again.

And it is all possible because in our weakest moments of unfaithfulness to our spouses and to Him, He remains faithful to us.

Pride

Pride goes before destruction,
a haughty spirit before a fall.

Proverbs 16:18

We all go through mountains and valleys in our journeys with God. At times, we are on the mountaintop, on fire for Him. We're searching and listening and seeing Him everywhere. Other times, we are in the valley and feel dry. We go days without praying, weeks without reading Scripture. We never hear from Him. I had begun a mountain trek months before the emotional affair had begun.

The summer before the affair happened, I began to get serious about making changes in my life. Scott and I were not doing well but I was tired of continuing in the way I acted. I made a list of the areas that I felt needed work within myself. I still have the list in my journal. Judgment. Anger. Jealousy. Vanity. Lust. Greed. Fear. The list went on. I began looking these up in Scripture and writing down related Scripture. As I examined the list, I began seeing a root cause of my issues. I had a serious problem with pride. Imagine, little miss 2.5 with a pride issue. Ha! I should have seen that one coming. That's the funny thing about pride though. You can see it in everyone but yourself.

As I look back now I see God was trying to prepare me especially for the approaching season of temptation. I fully believe He was trying to alert me to the attacks Satan would begin throwing against me.

Unfortunately, my own selfish, prideful desires to begin and stay in this relationship overwhelmed the wisdom I knew I should follow. I failed in using God's word and His leading to ward off this temptation.

However, the time I had spent studying about pride did make my spirit alert and made it easier to address the issues after the fact. Hindsight is 20/20 so I can now share with you some of the biggest ways pride made chinks in my armor.

Pride says "look at me"

One of the things that continually drew me back to conversations with this person is quite simply that he fed my ego. I had just had Lexi a year before and my figure was, as you would guess, not what it had been pre-pregnancy. I can remember just a few months into the pregnancy, my hips were not fitting into the same pregnancy jeans I had worn with Emma. My body was changing even more than it had with my first child. Even after giving birth, I was nursing, so I knew not to try to go on any diets. Not that I had the energy or time to get to a gym anyway.

I nursed Lexi through the summer but by fall, when she was weaned, I was ready to get out and make some changes. I joined a gym for the first time in my life that October. I began going three or four times a week, quickly moving into hard-core cardio and muscle-toning classes. Working out gave me the motivation to eat healthier. Saying no to a Kit Kat was easier when I knew the calories would simply cancel out my hard work at the gym. Just a month or two into my workouts and the change started coming.

This guy began noticing, too. I won't lie, it felt good after several years of having babies and nursing that someone who knew me pre-pregnancy still found me attractive. I couldn't seem to hear enough about the progress I was making.

Because God had led me through the studies of pride that summer, I knew even in the moment my vanity was an issue. I wrote this in my journal just days before things began spinning out of control that December.

... my desire for his attention has gotten the best of me. And I know from my study that it is pride rearing its ugly head again ... who doesn't like to hear good stuff about themselves? But it's not what I'm called to do so I still must resist the pride in myself.

Obviously I failed. And this aspect of pride is the part that had me coming back for seconds and thirds to these intimate conversations even after my confession to Scott. Those "I need to tell you something" moments with Scott the following months were almost always started because of pride. If I had a bad day, whether or not it was related to Scott, I was so desperate for feelings of worthiness and love and beauty that I would turn to him. I knew if I turned the conversation to personal matters at all, he would respond. That would lead to other conversations that I was looking for but that I wasn't strong enough to stop. In fact, they only fueled my pride.

Even when I could see what I was doing, there's another aspect to pride that made cutting it at its core nearly impossible.

Pride says "I deserve it."

Part of me knew I was in a downward spiral, but I kept telling myself it was okay because I deserved it. Scott and I were not in a good place. Oh, he was enjoying my changing body and his temper was improving but overall we could not consistently stay in a positive cycle. I don't want to blame Scott for my vanity but at some level, I justified it because I felt like I was treated so poorly that I deserved the attention from someone. Yes, I had my faults, but I worked so hard as a wife and mother and I was getting almost zero in return. This was my way of saying, *you know, I'm worth more than you're treating me.*

Pride says "I can handle it."

I mentioned before that I had been very 2.5 in my life. Never had sin truly had me in its grasp. Shortly before all this started, I found myself in a conversation with a few other coworkers. They were exchanging stories of the worst things they'd ever done. As I listened, I tried to come up with something to contribute to the conversation. The only thing I could come up with was either toilet papering a friend's house in high school or a time I had betrayed a friend's secret. Those confessions wouldn't hold water with these guys. I even started to say something and the guys shushed me, knowing I had nothing of significance to contribute. I'm not saying I didn't have any sin; I just hadn't been in a pit yet.

I somehow believed at the time it was because I was a strong warrior for Christ. That whatever Satan had thrown at me to date I had effectively slashed with the Sword of the Spirit. That no matter what Satan would throw at me, I could manage. The scariest lie pride whispers is, "You can handle it." I guess in some ways I just believed that no matter where this situation led, that I could cope with it on my own. I could figure out how to skirt questions from Scott. I could close my heart enough against the compliments and conversations. I could stop whatever train we were on without a second thought. How wrong I was. The truth of the matter is I was very weak. Just a simple compliment and I was turned to mush.

The thing about pride is it turns a person completely inward. Everything becomes about self. Pride is the very antithesis of being Christ-like. James 4:6 says, "God opposes the proud and gives grace to the humble." When we take our eyes off Christ and begin focusing on ourselves, suddenly we can't get enough. We become greedy with *more me. Yes, please tell me more about me. Yes, I deserve what he's telling me. Yes, I can do it all.* And the more we feed it, the more our pride builds. Pride is a green monster of itself and it only produces destruction. In my Life Application Study Bible in the book of Proverbs, it notes the results of pride that Proverbs alludes to:

- Leads to disgrace *11:2*
- Produces quarrels *13:10*
- Leads to punishment *16:5*
- Leads to destruction *16:18*
- Ends in downfall *18:12*
- Brings one low *29:23*

Every single one of those on the list has proven true in my life. I have been disgraced, punished, made low. Pride destructed my marriage, created fights, ended in a downfall of that relationship and the trust in my marriage.

I can't help but think again of King David. I mentioned in the last chapter how David's psalms connected with me so much in his grief over his sin. I also imagine that his struggles with Bathsheba and Uriah all started with a similar pride.

We know David was handsome in his youth. When Saul was choosing between Jesse's sons in 1 Samuel 16 it says that David was "ruddy, with a fine appearance and handsome features." As we follow David's life through 1st and 2nd Samuel, we see David as he slays the Philistine giant, escapes Saul's hands, becomes King of Judah and leads many military victories.

When we get to 2 Samuel 11, we drop into David's life one spring just as his men head off to war. One evening, David gets out of bed, goes onto his roof and sees a beautiful woman bathing. I can't help but think about David's thoughts at that moment. *"I'm a handsome man. I've been working awfully hard restoring peace to this great nation. I'm king, for crying out loud and there's a beautiful woman. I certainly deserve to have her company. I think I'll send someone after her."*

After he sleeps with Bathsheba, who happened to be married, she becomes pregnant. I can't help but think that at this point, his pride is telling him that he can figure it out. He then concocts a plan to have her husband Uriah killed in the line of duty. As king, he has no trouble succeeding. He has now committed adultery and murder.

See, David forgot God. And that's what pride does to all of us. We begin focusing on ourselves and our own circumstances and forget that God was the one got us to that point. We forget to give Him thanks. We forget to seek Him out. We forget that we are nothing without Him. We forget to humble ourselves.

Luke 14:11 states "For everyone who exalts himself will be humbled, and he who humbles himself will be exalted." When our pride takes over and we try to exalt ourselves, God takes it upon himself to humble us. He never lets us continue in our pride. Sometimes this means we see our pride for what it is and others, we are humbled in ways we wish we never encountered.

God used a prophet named Nathan to show David his sin. God tells David through Nathan he is the one who allowed him to succeed and would have given him more had that not been enough. And still, David killed Uriah and took Bathsheba as his wife. The Lord humbles him by giving his wives to someone else and letting his son, that was born of Bathsheba, die. I love what God says in 2 Samuel 12:12, "You did it in secret, but I will do this thing in broad daylight before all Israel." We cannot escape God. He detests pride and will bring us low until we learn this lesson.

Coming through this time has laid me very low. I have never been humbled as much as I was through this experience, and even now. Writing this book humbles me. I realize that I don't deserve anything that God gives me. I know that He is the one that has provided anything good that has come out of my life. I realize my total dependence on Him. I know that I don't have it all figured out and I'm desperate for His guidance. My heart has turned towards the needs of others instead of my own. It takes bowing before the Lord and giving Him due praise and thanks to find who we truly ought to be.

After so many times of failing Scott and having to admit failure after another failure, my pride, as you can imagine, had taken a beating. Yes, it was built up during the flirty conversations but it was quickly slashed when I would confess. Over time, I found that the good I felt was not worth what I dealt with afterward. Feeling good about myself became less important than feeling good in front of my husband and Father.

Never before have I known such contentment as I have since then. When I humble myself before the Lord instead of seeking man's praise, He lifts me up and sets me on solid ground. That feeling of worthiness and pride from our Heavenly Father is far more precious than anything man can give us.

Although, knowing how to humble yourself when you're not humble can be tough. However, maybe some of the ways pride manifested itself through my emotional affair resonate with you. If God has not already used this stretch of time to humble you Himself, there are some things I believe you can do to begin doing it on your own.

Acknowledge God's supremacy.

When pride is stripped away, we are left with a full dependency on God. We must acknowledge that God's way is the right way. We show that to God by looking to Him for our direction and fulfillment. When we are humble, we begin looking to Him before making any decisions. When we are feeling empty, we look to Him, knowing he has the power to help us. We stop saying we can figure it out and truly depend on Him for direction. Practically, you will begin seeking God in your Bible trying to find truths that relate to your circumstances. You will also find you are in prayer for His direction much more. Pride makes us turn inward but humility makes us turn upward.

Seek contentment and thankfulness.

When we are humble, our lives become less about how great we think we are or how much we deserve and more about how much God has already done for us. To remain humble, you need to be content in our current situations and always thanking him for bringing us to that place. Maybe your husband doesn't treat you well but at least you have a chance to work on your relationships. Maybe you have wonderful children He has given you to be thankful for. Certainly you have a roof over your head, clothes on your back and food to eat. This may be a hard time in your life but think of all the good times you have had until now. Just the fact that you are reading this shows that you are in the top percentage of wealth in the world. We have so much to be thankful for even when our lives are not perfect.

Worship is the key to showing God our thankfulness. People worship in different ways. Some write out things to be thankful for, others sing praises; still others will paint or create something as an act of worship. Truly humble people are constantly trying to give back to God for what He's already done.

View others as better than ourselves.

Philippians 2:3 says, "Do nothing out of selfish ambition or vain conceits, but in humility consider others better than yourselves." I learned the hard way through this that I looked down on others that had failed. My pride wouldn't let me see that I was just as capable of being in their situations.

During the past years, I have witnessed several celebrities go through public divorce after adultery. Tiger Woods, John Edwards, Mark Sanford, Arnold Schwarzenegger. Can I tell you that I have found such compassion for these people? I know what they did was wrong. I do. I have to realize that their extramarital relationships probably started a lot like mine. Only by the grace of God was I spared something worse.

When we become humble we consider others as better than ourselves. We all are sinners and we all have the ability to fail. So let us bind together and learn from each other. Proverbs 13:10 says, "Pride only breeds quarrels, but wisdom is found in those who take advice." We should begin looking to others and see what we can learn from them. Could you learn something from a woman who has cheated on five husbands? Could you learn something from someone who has murdered? While pride says we are better than those sinners, I think in their regrets are invaluable life lessons.

And yes, of course, we can learn from spiritual giants. They have been able to put into practice many of God's truths to become those people to us. The point is, when we are humble, we realize we are not better than anyone. We have a compassion for others and desire to connect with people than we did not have before.

Practically, we should begin seeking out truths that align with God's word from others. Begin listening to people you may have not listened to before. Seek out others' advice. Be ready to soak up the wisdom around you.

Pride is an ugly beast and can lead down so many destructive paths. In my life, it was the biggest chink in my armor that led me to my emotional affair. David said in Psalms 34:18, "The LORD is close to the brokenhearted and saves those who are crushed in spirit". The great news is it is never too late to give up our pride. Simply confess it and begin taking steps to humble yourself before him. And watch His beautiful grace on display as he draws nigh unto you. May it be so.

Deceit

Be self-controlled and alert.
Your enemy the devil prowls around like a roaring lion
   looking for someone to devour.
1 Peter 5:8

Someone, somewhere does not want me to write this chapter. Maybe even a little of me. This chapter is about truth. Truth is powerful. Truth changes people. I heartily believe this chapter could be such an eye-opener that it changes not just this situation you are in but it could change your life. And I don't say that lightly. It's simple, really: I'm going to speak truth. But before I speak some truth, I need to speak about lies.

I was very deceitful during my emotional affair. One can do this without telling direct lies. Sometimes we give ourselves a pass as long as no lies are told. The Ten Commandments say Thou Shalt Not Lie, not Thou Shalt Not Be Deceptive, right? Other times we assume a deceitful person is someone that covers up a bad situation with lies. But I am convinced that lying and being deceptive are two different things, both unacceptable in their own rights. I see it like this:

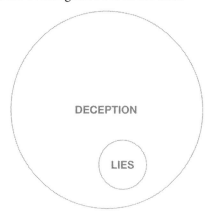

Psalm 120:2 says, "Save me, O LORD, from lying lips, and from deceitful tongues." Lying and deceitfulness are not the same. The original Hebrew, like English, has two different words for lying and deceitful. Lying is the Hebrew word sheqer which not surprisingly means lie, deception, disappointment, falsehood. Deceitful though is from the Hebrew noun rěmiyahi which has a broader definition: laxness, slackness, slackening, deceit, treachery. I find those words laxness, slackness, slackening fascinating. If you'd asked me to define deceit prior to looking it up, I surely wouldn't think of what essentially amounts to laziness. The Gesenius' Lexicon actually says to be slack or remiss and points to Proverbs 12:24 as an example. "The hand of the diligent shall bear rule: but the slothful shall be under tribute." (KJV) That word slothful is the same word Hebrew word rěmiyahi. So we have this picture of someone physically working hard in contrast to someone who is slothful, or lazy.

I think back to many question-and-answer sessions with Scott during this time of deception. Did I lie? No, but was I slothful, slack or remiss in my answers? Certainly. A simple question from him about what I did for lunch would be answered with "We went out to Chili's". I would be remiss in mentioning the "we" meant just me and this guy. The question "What are you doing up this late?" would be answered with "browsing the Internet". I was very slack in mentioning that "browsing" included chatting with this guy for hours on end. No lies escaped my lips but, I was being deceptive. I wanted him to think what was going on was a lot different than what actually was going on. I wanted a one-on-one lunch to look like a big, well-accepted group lunch with my coworkers. I wanted a one on one chat session to appear like I might be writing a blog post or checking email.

I think we do this naturally. Jeremiah 17:9 says, "The heart is deceitful above all things and desperately wicked, who can know it." If you have children, you can probably attest to the art of deception even at a young age. If I call back to my kids' room asking what they're doing and they are coloring their Barbies' faces with Sharpie and giving them a bath in a bowl of water they aren't supposed to have, their answer to me is going to be "playing with Barbies". Not a falsehood, or *sheqer*, but yes, a deception, *rĕmiyahi*. They are allowing the situation to appear better than it is. The deceitful heart rules until we learn truth is better.

Job 15:35 states, "They conceive mischief, and bring forth vanity, and their belly prepareth deceit". (KJV) Don't you relate to that "their belly prepareth deceit". It's that feeling in the pit of your stomach the moment when your husband asks one of those direct questions. Your belly churns and you start trying to think of a way not to lie but to get out of it without him knowing the real truth. It's interesting to me that Job brings up vanity. It's that pride again. Pride doesn't want someone else to know the truth of who we really are and what we're doing. Pride breeds deceit.

You might think you're getting away with being remiss but I submit God isn't dismissing it. Psalms 101:7 says, "He that worketh deceit [rĕmiyahi] shall not dwell within my house. Psalms 5:6 says, the LORD will abhor the bloody and deceitful [rĕmiyahi] man." (KJV) It's hard to hear but God *abhors* when you don't tell the full truth. He says he won't let us in His house.

I realize, if asked, we would agree not telling the whole truth is not good. But I want you to really see that saying "I never lied" is no excuse. We are called upon, as our American court systems demand, to tell the truth, the whole truth and nothing but the truth. God accepts nothing less.

When we have confessed and begin our road of repentance, we must begin telling truth. No lies and no deception. Do not be slack in your speech. Don't answer with the easy answer. Let us be diligent and work hard in our communication with those around us.

Deception is the first sin we see in the Bible. Adam and Eve might be the most retold story of the Old Testament. Of course we know the Genesis story of the serpent convincing Eve to eat of the forbidden tree in the garden, but I want to go back to it. I'll drop us right in right after the serpent beings to tempt Eve.

The woman said to the serpent, "We may eat fruit from the trees in the garden, but God did say, 'You must not eat fruit from the tree that is in the middle of the garden, and you must not touch it, or you will die.'"

"You will not certainly die," the serpent said to the woman. "For God knows that when you eat from it your eyes will be opened, and you will be like God, knowing good and evil."

Satan outright lies, saying they won't die but moreover, he continues giving them reasoning why his statement makes sense. It's as if he pretends to know just as much as God and says, "I know he said that, but the real reason he said it is this. So see, he didn't really mean it." Eve takes that and begins mulling it over and realizing that yeah, that kind of makes sense and actually, this whole thing could be good for me. And then she ropes Adam into her sin. Satan does not force her to sin, he just feeds her a lie to start her down her own path of selfish actions.

Here's the thing. Satan cannot make us sin. But he has no qualms about lying or being deceptive to make us do it on our own accord. He is the ultimate deceiver and liar. Jeremiah 29:11 tells us that God has plans for us. "For I know the plans I have for you," declares the LORD, "plans to prosper you and not to harm you, plans to give you hope and a future." Well, Satan's got plans too. I took a look in the Bible at all the times Satan was mentioned and these are some phrases attached to him. Satan:

- Stood up
- Provoked
- Came along
- Went to and fro
- Walked up and down
- Tempted
- Came immediately

Those are mentions in just a handful of verses. Satan is a busy person. He is doing anything and everything to undo every single thing that God is trying to do in your life. He wants to control your marriage, your children, your church, your job, your home, your security, your love, your compassion, your joy and most of all your faith. He is running around like a chicken with its head cut off trying to lie and deceive his way into tricking us into sin. Because sin destroys.

I think the most effective deceptive tool he has is not to get us to lie to others or deceive others but to deceive ourselves. In other words, like Eve, we start buying his lies and taking them for truth. Unlike when someone else deceives us, there is no one to trip up and let the truth come out. We keep replaying the lies in our mind and no one knows the difference. Our own evil desires take care of the rest. All of those justifications I listed a few chapters back were complete and utter lies which I told myself, which in turn launched me into this emotional affair.

Because I was being so deceptive, no one knew what was going on and there was no one to speak truth into my life. My mother is one of my best friends and even if I don't tell her what's going on, she usually figures it out. She is one of the wisest people I know and always the one I go to for a gut check. She has no qualms about speaking truth into my life. Because I was so ashamed of what I had done, I did not breathe a word of this to her until the first draft of this book was written. In doing so, I cut off that line of wisdom that usually spoke truth into my life. In fact, I cut off everyone. The only hope I had was in the Holy Spirit.

I mentioned before how much I felt conviction during this time. The Holy Spirit was pushing me back to God. He was trying to say, "Hey, listen to me, wake up. That stuff Satan is feeding you is a lie. Pay attention, listen to me, I have the truth." He was pushing me back to God so I could open my eyes from the deception I had bought into myself.

Perhaps you are buying into some of those same justifications I did. While I can never replace the work the Holy Spirit (or your mother) can do in your life, I'd like to speak a little truth.

- Your actions are not pretend. It is real. The conversations are real. The looks are real. The lust is real.
- The path you are on will lead you to a physical affair. You must get off before this happens.
- You are to have a clean heart and conversation above reproach.
- You are not helping one another move towards Christ. You are tearing down His work.
- You are cheating on your husband.
- He is not your soul mate. If you are married, your husband is your soul mate.
- Your behavior with this person is irrelevant to your husband's issues. You alone are responsible for your sin.
- You are not just friends. You have attached your heart to his.
- You do not have enough room to love both people in an intimate way. God designed marriage to be intimate, emotionally and physically, with one person.

These are truths to my justifications. Satan was trying to make something look different than it was. A destructive relationship disguised itself as two spiritual accountability partners. An illicit conversation were just two people playing pretend. My husband's anger seemed a good reason to commit deception. I bought into the lies and agreed with his reasoning. Maybe you have a different list. Add your own truths. Ask God to open your eyes.

One last way I believe Satan keeps you trapped even after you have ended the relationship is by making you feel shame. Shame and sorrow are different things. Sorrow is regret for what you've done but as we've discussed, it leads to humbleness and joy. When you humble yourself and confess, your sorrow leads to God lifting you up. Shame is a lie that Satan deceives you with that tells you you cannot tell anyone what has happened; you are the only one to ever feel this way people will turn away from you; you have to keep the truth of what you've done hidden. Shame only beats you down and keeps things hidden even more.

James 5:15 says, "Therefore confess your sins to each other and pray for each other so that you may be healed." There is something powerful and healing about confessing our sins to other believers. They are able to come alongside you and lift you up in prayer.

Furthermore, we are to show others the comfort that we have received from God. I think it is Satan's tactic to keep our sins hidden, particularly when we've decided to fight against them. As long as he can keep us hidden, alone and struggling, we will be all the more ineffective for Christ. The sooner we can share our own struggles and comfort others in the same struggle, the stronger we will be together.

Satan is striking hard from so many directions. He is truly fighting as hard as he can with his lies to not only entice and entangle you but to keep you from helping others untangle themselves. Open your eyes, beg God for the truth and fight back. Truth changes people. I know it can change you.

Love

Theme Song:

How He loves, The David Crowder Band

A flower, watered by the rain, grew on the side of the riverbank. When the rain stopped, it reached through its roots to the river. The flower bloomed like never before. In time, the river dried up and the flower wilted until the rain came back gently. However, the flower was the same as the others now, never blooming as it once had when fed by the river water.

That was the gist of a metaphorical short story I wrote the year after my affair ended. It defined how I felt about what had happened. Scott had been providing what I needed to survive. When his "love" felt like it ended, I started looking elsewhere to survive. This new person, the river, made me feel like I never had before. But that was temporary. Scott eventually began pouring his love out again and I could bloom once more. At the time I wrote the story, I just knew I would never feel complete.

But I had this all wrong. So wrong. The problem was not so much that I turned to another person for my needs. The problem started way before my emotional affair. The problem was that I was looking to a person to meet my needs at all. You were not made to love a man. God created you to love Him and for you to love Him back. That's it. He will fulfill every single need that you have. Are we supposed to love other people? Absolutely! But if we are looking from person to person to ultimately fulfill our needs, we will never feel satisfied.

I find it fascinating that I used a metaphor about plants years ago to describe relationships. Jesus used a different one, one that recently showed me how I really was supposed to function.

In John 15, Jesus says that He is a vine and God is the gardener. We are branches of the vine. He says when we do not remain connected to Him as the vine, we can do nothing. He says it's as if we wither and die and are then thrown into a fire. We are dead inside. But he also says if we remain in His love by obeying his commandments, our joy will be complete. Jesus is how we are nourished. We do not experience true, joyful, soul-filling love unless we remain attached to the source of love.

Now, what's interesting is He turns right around in the next verse and commands us to "Love one another as I have loved you". See, we love each other only through His love. When we do it on our own and start looking to other people to fill us up, it is as if we die inside. That is how these feelings become an obsession that is never satisfied. We look and look for a person to finally make us feel that love that we are designed to feel. But when we finally do connect to the right source, it is as if we have an internal love bucket that begins to overflow. Our hearts our full. Our minds are at peace. And then a really cool thing happens. Suddenly, we feel this overwhelming desire to love other people in a Godly way. 1 John 4:10-11 states, "Herein is love, not that we loved God, but that he loved us, and sent his Son to be the propitiation for our sins. Beloved, if God so loved us, we ought also to love one another." It is in the abundance of His love that we are able to love people the right way. If we try to rely on our own strength, we muck it up and find ourselves in relationships that not only don't fill us up but sometimes destruct everything around us.

When I look back at what happened, I can clearly see that what I was searching for in my husband and what I went after in this relationship were simply my heart's cry for God's love. He alone can fully satisfy my desire to be loved, desired, appreciated, enjoyed, protected, forgiven, heard and known.

Now, as I mentioned at the first of the book, I've been a church girl my whole life. I knew God loved me and I loved Him. My entire life, I desperately sought His face. But I've figured out I compartmentalized my love sources. One source was my spiritual one that I knew came from God but the other was my human source of love. It's as if I was saying, "Ok God, we are good. I know you love me and I love you. Now, let's go figure out this romance thing and then I'll feel protected and appreciated and beautiful and desired." What I've since realized is that there is one source of love. We are the branch and He is the vine. He provides all the needs that we have. We should not be looking for people to meet them. Yes, it's wonderful if our husbands do desire us or protect us but if they do not, we are not left empty and devastated. We will be nourished by God and our fulfillment is already there.

The linchpin of this is remaining in Him. If remaining in Him is so important, how do we do it? In John 15:10, Jesus says, "If you obey my commands, you will remain in my love, just as I have obeyed my Father's commands and remain in his love." In John 14:21, Jesus says, "Whoever has my commands and obeys them, he is the one who loves me." In John 14:25, Jesus says, "He who does not love me will not obey my teaching." Sounds like a broken record, right? We love Christ through obedience. You know what that takes? Knowing God. We have to know what He expects of us in order to obey. And when we start studying His word and obeying it, a funny thing happens. We start seeing that His ways are higher than ours. Life starts working out a little better. Our relationships get cleaned up. Our attitudes get cleaned up. He gives us the desires of our heart. And when we see that His commands are good, we start falling in love with Him because He's taking care of us. He's so good to us! It makes us want to cycle back and learn more and then obey more and then yes, love more! It's a wonderful cycle to be in.

And let me tell you, I have discovered how deep, how rich, how wonderful His love is. And I'm not special. He feels this way about you. Allow me to share some special ways in which God knows and loves you.

- He knows you intimately
- He thinks you're beautiful
- He delights in you
- He will fight for you
- He forgives you
- He wants the best for you
- He listens to you
- He gave up his most precious son for you
- He thinks about you
- He protects you
- He offers gifts to you
- He wants to give you the desires of your heart
- He enjoys your singing and dancing
- He's patient with you
- He will never leave you
- He is jealous for you
- He loves you no matter what you do, or have done

Don't believe me? Let me show it.

He knows you intimately
Matthew 10:30 And even the hairs of your head are all numbered.

Psalm 94:11a The LORD knows the thoughts of man.

Jeremiah 1:5a Before I formed you in the womb I knew you, before you were born I set you apart.

He thinks you're beautiful

1 Timothy 4:4 For everything God created is good, and nothing is to be rejected if it is received with thanksgiving.

Ecclesiastes 3:1a He has made everything beautiful in its time.

Genesis 1:31a God saw all that he had made, and it was very good.

He delights in you

Proverbs 12:22 The LORD detests lying lips, but he delights in men who are truthful.

Psalm 147:11 The Lord delights in those who fear him, who hope their hope in his unfailing love.

Zephaniah 3:17 The LORD your God is with you, he is mighty to save.

He will take great delight in you, he will quiet you with his love.

He will fight for you

Exodus 14:14 The LORD will fight for you; you need only to be still.

Romans 8:3 Who is he that condemns? Christ Jesus, who died—more than that, who was raised to life—is at the right hand of God and is also interceding for us.

He forgives you

1 John 1:9 If we confess our sins, he is faithful and just to forgive us our sins, and to cleanse us from all unrighteousness.

Ephesians 1:7 In him we have redemption through his blood, the forgiveness of sins, in accordance with the riches of God's grace.

He wants the best for you

Jeremiah 29:11 "For I know the plans I have for you," declares the LORD, "plans to prosper you and not to harm you, plans to give you hope and a future.

He listens to you

1 Peter 3:12 For the eyes of the Lord are on the righteous and his ears are attentive to their prayer.

He sent His son to die for you

John 3:16 For God so loved the world that he gave his one and only Son, that whoever believes in him shall not perish but have eternal life.

Romans 8:32 He who did not spare his own Son, but gave him up for us all -- how will he not also, along with him, graciously give us all things?

He thinks about you

Psalm 139:17 How precious also are thy thoughts unto me, O God! how great is the sum of them! (KJV)

Psalm 40:5 Many, O LORD my God, are thy wonderful works which thou hast done, and thy thoughts which are to us-ward: they cannot be reckoned up in order unto thee: if I would declare and speak of them, they are more than can be numbered. (KJV)

Jeremiah 29:11 For I know the thoughts that I think toward you, saith the LORD, thoughts of peace, and not of evil, to give you an expected end. (KJV)

He protects you

Psalm 50:15 Call upon Me in the day of trouble; I will deliver you, and you will honor Me.

Psalm 91:11 For he will command his angels concerning you to guard you in all your ways.

He offers gifts to you

John 10:28 I give them eternal life, and they shall never perish; no one can snatch them out of my hand.

Matthew 7:11 If you, then, though you are evil, know how to give good gifts to your children, how much more will your Father in heaven give good gifts to those who ask him!

He wants to give you the desires of your heart

Psalm 37:4 Delight yourself in the LORD and he will give you the desires of your heart.

Psalm 145:19 He fulfills the desires of those who fear him; he hears their cry and saves them.

He enjoys your singing and dancing

Colossians 3:16 Let the word of Christ dwell in you richly as you teach and admonish one another with all wisdom, and as you sing psalms, hymns and spiritual songs with gratitude in your hearts to God.

Ephesians 5:19 Speak to one another with psalms, hymns and spiritual songs. Sing and make music in your heart to the Lord.

Psalms 149:3 Let them praise his name with dancing and make music to him with tambourine and harp.

Psalm 150:4 Praise him with tambourine and dancing, praise him with the strings and flute.

He's patient with you

2 Peter 3:9 The Lord is not slow in keeping His promise, as some understand slowness. He is patient with you, not wanting anyone to perish, but everyone to come to repentance.

He will never leave you

Hebrews 10:23 Let us hold unswerving to the hope we profess, for He who promised is faithful.

He is jealous for you
2 Corinthians 11:2 I am jealous for you with a godly jealousy. I promised you to one husband, to Christ, so that I might present you as a pure virgin to him.

He loves you no matter what you do, or have done
Romans 8:38-39 For I am convinced that neither death nor life, neither angels nor demons, neither the present nor the future, nor any powers, neither height nor depth, nor anything else in all creation, will be able to separate us from the love of God that is in Christ Jesus our Lord.

I hope that takes your breath away. The God that created this whole universe cares so carefully for each one of us. If you really take a look at the traits that could easily be a list of qualities we seek in our spouses. But please, I hope you are seeing that those are things that can and should be fulfilled by God. He created you just so He could satisfy all those longings. He wants so badly to do it. Won't you let him?

SECTION IV

THE ABIDING

As I close the last section on the spiritual truths God taught me, I want to look toward the future of your marriage. This section will deal with practical ways in which my marriage was spared.

Marriage

Theme Song:
Beautiful Things, Gungor

N ot until recently could I fathom Paul's recommendation in 1 Corinthians 7:8 to stay single. Being affirmed and loved by a man was one of my ultimate desires. I can't tell you how much I wanted that fairy tale story from the movies and novels I was always engrossing myself in.

After learning how God truly meets my needs, I am finally able to see singleness as a possibility. Now, don't get me wrong, I'm not regretting marriage or saying one shouldn't get married. Marriage is a beautiful picture of Christ and his church. All I'm saying is healing can come with or without your husband. True healing is between you and God. But the fact is, I am married and in order to make our marriage look like Christ and the church, Scott and I had some work to do.

I've walked you through my story to the point of confession and the spiritual truths that were revealed over the past years. Along the way, though, our marriage has healed as well. I have a vertical relationship with Christ that needed to be fixed but I also had this horizontal marital relationship to work on. While I'm no marital counselor, I learned some practical things that helped our marriage work post-emotional affair.

Commit

I talked about this in *A Choice*, but it bears repeating. Marriage is a decision. A commitment. A covenant. Without your decision for your marriage to last, it will not.

I am a blessed woman with a husband that is strong in his faith. We both agreed we would commit to our marriage. I'm not sure the words were ever spoken but we knew we were in this for the long haul. The point is: we both knew divorce was not an option.

You might say, "Well, that's fine, but my spouse could care less about this marriage; why do you think I had this emotional affair in the first place?" But let me say something that may surprise you. You do not need to wait for your spouse to agree the marriage should be saved. If you want to save your marriage, you commit to saving your marriage. I have seen several couples where one person was halfway out the door but the other worked so hard on him or herself and the relationship that the one leaving stopped short. He or she took a step back inside and said, "Wait a minute. What's that I see you doing in there?" But there has to be that commitment from at least one person to say "I'm going to fight for this". If your marriage is going to fail, please do not let it be because you do not fight hard enough. God is on your side. He sees you as one person and does not wish you to separate. If you are still married, it is not too late. Marriage does take two to last but sometimes it only takes one to step out in faith and salvage it. Be the one.

Confess and forgive

I got an email reply from one of my mentors shortly after my confession to Scott. I mentioned things weren't great and she agreed to meet me almost immediately for coffee to talk. She was the first person aside from my husband that I told what had happened. At that time, I was still defending the relationship, trying not to make a big deal of it. I half-heartedly explained the relationship as a few errant conversations. I believe she could see through what I was getting at and I remember her saying something to the effect of, "God gave you a test and you failed."

I bristled at that and just wanted to say, "He's just a friend! I haven't failed at anything!" As tears rolled down my cheeks, though, I knew my situation was serious. Although Scott knew what was going on at this point, there was something about hearing that I had failed from a respected mentor that really infused the seriousness of my transgressions. Confession humbled me but most importantly it was another step in pushing me towards healing.

Just a few months later, we had a speaker come to our church to conduct a women's conference. She offered a few slots during the afternoon for private counseling. I wasn't sure what she could do in just a few minutes, but I knew I needed to be in one of those slots.

I could feel the lump in my throat as I sat in one of our pastor's offices that she had claimed for the afternoon. The lump quickly turned to tears. I cried as I poured my heart out while she took notes on a legal pad, nodding as if she'd heard the story a thousand times. She asked, "Is your husband harsh?" I nodded vigorously. She nodded as she heard the answer she expected and wrote some more. As I finished talking, she stopped writing, looked at me and said, "This is what needs to happen." She then gave me this advice, which I will extend to you. Each of you needs to write a list of offenses you have committed against the other person. Do not write a list of offenses your spouse has performed against you. Take your lists to each other, read them aloud and then ask for forgiveness from each other.

My husband and I did this and I could barely speak I was crying so hard. Even though I could make a list a mile long of ways he had offended me, I realized that I was every bit as guilty of contributing to problems in our marriage, even barring the affair. That started a process of confessing and forgiving. Again and again. Communication and forgiveness is the absolute key to our commitment.

Talk to someone

I told you of my meeting with my mentor and the counselor first to suggest you do as the counselor suggested and second to say sometimes you just need someone with whom to talk. There is something powerful about looking someone in the eye and speaking truth. I am reminded of the creation story when God simply speaks the earth into existence. Words are powerful.

While Scott and I never did go to couples therapy, I'd highly recommend you do. It can't hurt and it most likely will help. If for whatever you reason you can't get to one or afford therapy, be sure to reach out to your local churches. I know of a local counselor that only charges what the couple can afford. I will advise you, though, to specifically look for a Christian counselor that does not recommend divorce as a general rule. While I do believe there are instances where divorce might be acceptable, you are likely not going to gain any help from someone that pushes for a divorce if your differences seem irreconcilable. I wholeheartedly believe and am proof that a marriage can reconcile after an emotional affair and have seen other couples that dealt with physical affairs thrive as well.

Find an accountability partner. You need a Godly woman who will listen and speak truth into your life. My girlfriends are my bedrock. I am sure I talked about this more times than I can count. I never did meet with my mentor or that counselor again but I was able to relay my struggles to my girlfriends. Just getting it out sometimes, even vaguely was enough to propel me in the right direction again. We cannot do this alone. Please don't try.

Open your life but guard your heart

I've talked about ending my relationship with the other person as much as I could, given our circumstances. We still were on the same team at work and had to communicate, so I needed to make some changes in order to protect my marriage.

Foremost, Scott was open and welcome to view all chat sessions, emails, text messages, social media accounts, etc. I could not protest if he asked to see them. More importantly, I proactively showed him any conversations that were even questionable. Take it upon yourself to divulge what's going on. This removes the discomfort of your spouse seeming like a prying parent. Putting away childish things include trying not to hide conversations. If you want your marriage to work, you have to divulge the truth, the whole truth and nothing but the truth. But on your own. Don't wait until he asks. I remember a few times I would be mid-conversation, and I would stop to show Scott my screen so he could give me a suggestion on how to respond appropriately. Realize that you are back on the same team and you are guarding your marriage together.

We also agreed on practical rules such as no chatting with males past 10 p.m. or no lunches alone with the opposite sex. These will look different for each couple, and the guidelines can always change after you're back on solid ground. Rules may make you feel like a wayward teenager; but unfortunately, the shoe fits.

Most of the changes, though, have not altered just how I act but also how I think. When I receive compliments, I am grateful but I don't internalize them like I used to. I try to keep my pride in check and remember that my fulfillment comes from God alone. I also try not to internalize Scott's bad moods. I remember that God loves me, He is faithful, He appreciates me; and my mood and attitude is not dependent on how Scott is feeling. Memorizing and repeating Scripture is so helpful at this point. If you are getting complimented, recite verses on pride. If you are in a fight, recite verses on love. What you'll find is when your heart changes, your actions change naturally.

It's a personal thing

About a year after this happened we realized that Scott's issues were more than we could handle. The way he would get upset over small issues didn't seem normal. He visited his primary physician and as we had suspected, we found out he does have a slight case of Obsessive Compulsive Disorder. While he's not dealing with issues as obvious as flipping light switches 30 times in a row, his body has a hard time processing disorder. His doctor prescribed him an antidepressant, which has done wonders for both of us. I call it my happy medicine. He is now able to control his impulses to lash out. While the medicine was not a panacea for all of our problems, it finally put us on even playing ground so we could build up our marriage together.

I also find that I've become more patient with him when I know he hasn't had his medicine or if we're having a particularly messy day at the house. Simply the awareness that he's having a chemical, not emotional, reaction to his environment has helped me respond appropriately.

Please, if you are seeing personality issues in yourself or your spouse that are causing problems, do not hesitate to see a doctor. Any of these issues may have chemical origins and it's possible they are not spiritual or emotional at all. Your marriage is probably suffering the most because you are the first line of offense.

And that brings me to what I want to say next that may be a surprise to you as it was to me. Andy Stanley, pastor of North Point in Atlanta, said this in a sermon: you do not have marital problems. Marital issues are how to squeeze the toothpaste and which way the toilet roll goes on the holder. The truth is you are two people, with issues, trying to live together. But issues that result in an emotional affair are far deeper and relate on an individual level. I had my pride, my unfaithfulness and my love all messed up. Scott had some medical things to work through. Our marriage was not so much broken as we were. And are. We all are messed up in our own ways and at different times we'll be each struggling through different issues. The thing is, we always need to be working to make a better version of ourselves. Be careful that you are not making your spouse a better version of themselves. While Genesis tells us we are our spouse's help meets, God tells us in Matthew 7:5 to take the plank out of our own eyes first. We have lots to work on. Let's concentrate on that.

Learn to relate

While we are working on ourselves, we do have ways in which we can learn to relate to our spouses better. There are a few concepts I've read in a couple of books that have absolutely helped our marriage for the better.

"Love Languages"

The first book I recommend may be familiar to you: Gary Chapman's The 5 Love Languages. Chapman says each of us gives and receives love in distinct ways but all the ways all boil down to five categories: touch, words of affirmation, time, acts of service and receiving gifts. We all love in all these ways but are prone to give and receive it in one or two ways most often.

My top two love languages are acts of service and words of affirmation. If you give me a compliment, I could live off of it for days. On the flip side, negative comments could affect me for years. I often feel loved when Scott mows the grass or builds me a shelf I designed. On the flip side, laziness makes me crazy. The other love languages are less effective for me. You could go years without getting me a gift and I would be A-OK. In fact, Scott and I normally don't exchange presents on birthdays or anniversaries. We buy something for each other for Christmas only so the kids can see us giving each other gifts.

As you can tell, Scott's language isn't receiving gifts either. Scott's love language is touch. He is deeply hurt when I forget to kiss or hug him hello. Often if we are fighting, simply reaching out to hold his hand will be enough of an apology.

These languages help us to better communicate love to our spouses. Perhaps before the affair your husband was trying to tell you in his language how he loved you, and you were missing it. I know that I tend to work hard around the house thinking that if I do enough laundry that he will really know that I love him when all the while all he wants for me is to sit with him on the couch and scratch his back. Our marriage can be on a positive cycle but may not reach its full potential if we don't love each other the right way.

Another key reason to understanding your love language is it could explain a root cause of your emotional affair. I realized my emotional affair began when this person began meeting my top two love languages: acts of service and words of affirmation. He was doing something for me and complimenting me. At the same time, Scott was tearing me down with his words. This man was filling the exact gap that had been created between me and Scott.

Perhaps your love language is quality time and your husband travels for work a lot and an old boyfriend from high school keeps you company online while he's away. The scenarios are endless but search out first your love languages and take a good look to see how they fit into these relationships.

I have to be very careful when someone compliments me or does anything for me. I internalize that as love and sometimes it gets me into trouble. Be aware of each other's love languages and use them to your benefit in your marriage.

"Love and Respect"

The other book I recommend is Dr. Emerson Eggerich's Love and Respect. Dr. Eggerich named this vicious cycle that I kept seeing between myself and Scott, The Crazy Cycle. And boy does it feel crazy when you're in it. Everything is going great or everything is unhinged. He pinpoints for women what is likely causing men to fall into the Crazy Cycle and that is a lack of respect. I realized I can love Scott all I want in the right language but if I disrespect him in the least, all of it is for naught. He immediately shuts down and that adds fuel to the fire. On the other hand, husbands have to remember to love their wives like Christ loves the church. And that means being a humble servant. We treat our spouses like Kings and they treat us like precious Queens from the perspective of servants. If we both act in humbleness but get treated like royalty, we both get the fairy tale we're after.

In summary, here are some steps you can take to move forward:

- Decide to commit
- Seek out a mentor or friend
- See a counselor
- See a medical doctor
- Confess and forgive offenses
- Guard your heart and mind
- Be open with your communication
- Read Five Love Languages
- Read Love and Respect

As I close out this section, I want to be sure you continue to hear that first and foremost your spiritual healing is your priority. Lean into God, humble yourself and let God love you. He is the answer. He *is* the answer. While God continues the spiritual healing in you, make these practical steps towards healing with your spouse.

You Are More

Theme Song:

You Are More, Tenth Avenue North

The song mentioned above has absolutely haunted me during the past few months. I think I had come to believe that because of this emotional affair I was less-than. Although I deeply regret my choices, the truth is I am more than these choices. I've been making bad choices all of my life, these just happened to have tougher consequences. And no matter what bad choices I make, God redeems. He has saved me from them and I am not defined by those choices. This struggle is about God, not me. He's shown me that life only works with Him. He says I'm a child of the King. He says my sins are forgotten. He says He has plans for me. He says I'm worthy through Christ. My life is not a summation of these bad choices.

And you are more than any bad choices you might have made or any kind of mess you are in right now. You have the ability to write a different story for your life. You do not need to be stuck in a cycle of deceit, defeat or darkness. Just take the next right step. If you are still enjoying your emotional affair, pray that God will give you his desire to get out of Satan's deceptive hold. If you are in the midst of it and want out, make the decision now to confess to your husband and pry yourself out. You do have the power to do it in Christ's name. If you have experienced this in the past, my hope is that you know you are not defined by your mistakes. There is healing and we should live proudly in Christ's redemption.

Not only are you more than these choices, your marriage is too. Right now, faith and trust have been completely broken. Trust must be earned back as we continue to confess and communicate. But please hear me when I say trust can be earned back. While it seems impossible at the moment, healing is possible. Your marriage does not have to be defined by this moment.

God has been so gracious to me and Scott. Through all of this we have come out healthier and stronger. Yes, there are scars, but we made it. We celebrated 13 years of marriage the week that I wrote this chapter. We're in the process of adopting a son. Six years ago we wouldn't have dreamed of bringing another child into the mix. I think that speaks volumes for how far we have come.

You can do this. Your marriage is more than the sum of your mistakes. Don't you know who you are? What's been done for you? Cling to Christ. He's so faithful.

"Our Master Jesus has his arms wide open for you and I love all of you in Christ Jesus." (MSG) *1 Corinthians 16:23-24*

Afterward

After having several close friends read the book, over and over I heard the feedback that they wanted to hear Scott's point of view. And I agreed. It's one thing to be the person that experienced an emotional affair but it's quite another to be the spouse of that person. But problems abounded in his sharing. This was and is still painful for him. It's not something we openly talk about often. I mentioned earlier in the book that we still have scars. This time in our lives is a sore spot. When I told him I was planning to write this book, I was clear I didn't want to write it but felt God's strong prompting. He gave it his blessing and then again after he read the book.

The other reason I never thought we'd get his point of view is Scott simply abhors writing. I gently prompted him after each person suggested it and just days before the book was complete, with great shock and appreciation, I received a full page of response from Scott to share.

What I love about what he says is he reiterates a lot of what you've already read. While it may feel redundant, it does my heart good to know we're on the same page. The bottom line is that God is the one that salvaged our marriage, not our own efforts. I hope this is a blessing for you.

My side of the story.   By Scott Bennett

I really don't like to share it because it's embarrassing. However, I know that sometimes our pain can bring help and healing to others.

I have always known that I have a way about me that requires things to be in order, neat, clean and in line. I seem to get worse the older I get. I look back and recall all the times I was out of line with Amy when I would blow up. I would come home from work and the house would be a "disaster". In truth, it was only simply in. I would make statements that were mean, hurtful and painful. Those are not excuses for what Amy did; we all have to own up to our mistakes. But I will be the first to admit I did not make things easy for her. I nearly severed our emotional ties to each other. I was not there for her to lean on and I was not there to take care of her.

Before I knew what was going on, I started looking at her emails out of the blue. It's still a mystery to me why. God knew what was going on even when I didn't. I started reading late-night emails that triggered my attention. After a while I would look more often and read more and more to see what was going on. I never read anything that pointed to an affair but just the fact that someone else was talking to Amy that late at night was enough to make me wonder. I do not recall what made me finally ask Amy what was going on; however, I do remember that day. I asked her about the emails and if there was anything going on between them that I needed to know about. I also asked if there were more conversations that I would not like. She told me there were and I started drilling her for information. After getting all the information I was extremely mad and disappointed in Amy and our relationship.

I had thoughts of getting the guy in trouble at his and Amy's workplace or having a talk with him. I would have liked to have some time alone with him. However, I knew that this was a spiritual battle we were facing and nothing I did in those terms would make things better. I let Amy know that I had lost all trust in her and I did not make things easy for her for a while afterward. I did not let her forget what she had done.

However, I never thought of divorce or even leaving Amy. Maybe because a man sees and feels things different than a woman, I never felt as if she committed the act of adultery. We both agree the Bible says it is adultery in her heart but I never felt as if she had cheated on me. Don't get me wrong, wrong is wrong and bad is bad. I was not happy and I was hurt but I was never at the point of throwing in the towel.

Before we were married, we agreed that divorce would never be an option for us. It took us a while to get where we are, and we will always be a work in progress. I can say that we are closer both to each other and to God more than ever. There is no doubt that God carried us through. We hope that God can use us and our lives to help others grow. God tells us we will never be alone and that he will give us what we need to get through the storms.

No one will be able to stand against you all the days of your life. As I was with Moses, so I will be with you; I will never leave you nor forsake you. *Joshua 1:5*

No temptation has overtaken you except what is common to mankind. And God is faithful; he will not let you be tempted beyond what you can bear. But when you are tempted, he will also provide a way out so that you can endure it. *1 Corinthians 10:13*

Acknowledgments

First and foremost, I'd like to thank Christ for His love so exquisite and His grip so secure. To my husband, for his unending forgiveness and faithfulness. To Carrie, for telling me the truth. To Shelley, for telling me years ago that this book had a chance. To Becky, Dani, Liz and Melissa, for listening to me over countless cups of coffee, emails and text messages. To my family, for their unending support. To Beth Moore, even though she doesn't know I exist. Her Bible studies and conferences changed me in ways she prayed they would. And finally to my blog readers at Permission to Peruse, for helping me find my voice.

About the Author

Amy Bennett is a recovering perfectionist and lover of God. She is wife to her police officer husband, Scott, and mommy to two beautiful girls, Emma and Lexi, and hopefully one handsome boy soon. They reside in South Carolina, in a suburb of Charlotte, North Carolina, with their two dogs, Mattie and Tucker, and a picket fence to hold them all in. Amy spends her day writing code for a bank and her evenings writing blog posts at Permission to Peruse. You can find her on Twitter at @amyjbennett.

Resources

Playlist

- In This Life, Collin Raye
- Mine, Taylor Swift
- Slow Fade, Casting Crowns
- Somewhere in the Middle, Casting Crowns
- Haunted, Taylor Swift
- Need You Now, Lady Antebellum
- Before the Morning, Josh Wilson
- East to West, Casting Crowns
- How He Loves, The David Crowder Band
- Beautiful Things, Gungor
- You are More, Tenth Avenue North

Scripture Listing

Introduction

Praise be to the God and Father of our Lord Jesus Christ, the Father of compassion and the God of all comfort, who comforts us in all our troubles, so that we can comfort those in any trouble with the comfort we ourselves have received from God. *2 Corinthians 1:3-4*

Faith

His back has rows of shields
tightly sealed together;
each is so close to the next
that no air can pass between.
They are joined fast to one another;
they cling together and cannot be parted.
Job 41:15-17

My bone cleaveth to my skin and to my flesh. *Job 19:20 (KJV)*

Therefore shall a man leave his father and his mother, and shall cleave unto his wife: and they shall be one flesh." *Genesis 2:24 (KJV)*

'You have heard that it was said, 'Do not commit adultery.' But I tell you that anyone who looks at a woman lustfully has already committed adultery with her in his heart.' *Matthew 5:27-28*

Again and again I sent all my servants, the prophets, to you. They said, 'Each of you must turn from your wicked ways and reform your actions...' But you have not paid attention or listened to me. *Jeremiah 35:15*

But I tell you the truth: It is for your good that I [Jesus] am going away. Unless I go away, the Counselor will not come to you; but if I go, I will send him to you. When he comes, he will convict the world of guilt in regard to sin and righteousness and judgment. *John 16:7-8*

For a man's ways are in full view of the LORD, and he examines all his paths.
The evil deeds of a wicked man ensnare him;
the cords of his sin hold him fast.
He will die for lack of discipline,
led astray by his own great folly.
Proverbs 5:21-23

If we confess our sins, he is faithful and just and will forgive us our sins and purify us from all unrighteousness. *1 John 1:9*

Whoever conceals their sins does not prosper, but the one who confesses and renounces them finds mercy. *Proverbs 28:13*

For I know my transgressions, and my sin is always before me.
Against you, you only, have I sinned
and done what is evil in your sight;
so you are right in your verdict
and justified when you judge.
Surely I was sinful at birth,
sinful from the time my mother conceived me.
Yet you desired faithfulness even in the womb;
you taught me wisdom in that secret place.
Psalm 51:3-6

My guilt has overwhelmed me
like a burden too heavy to bear.
My wounds fester and are loathsome
because of my sinful folly.
I am bowed down and brought very low;
all day long I go about mourning.
My back is filled with searing pain;
there is no health in my body.
I am feeble and utterly crushed;
I groan in anguish of heart.

All my longings lie open before you, Lord;
my sighing is not hidden from you.
My heart pounds, my strength fails me;
even the light has gone from my eyes.

For I am about to fall,
and my pain is ever with me.
I confess my iniquity;
I am troubled by my sin.

LORD, do not forsake me;
do not be far from me, my God.
Come quickly to help me,
my Lord and my Savior.
Psalm 38:4-22

Find rest, O my soul, in God alone;
my hope comes from him.
He alone is my rock and my salvation;
he is my fortress, I will not be shaken.
My salvation and my honor depend on God;
he is my mighty rock, my refuge.
Trust in him at all times, O people;
pour out your hearts to him,
for God is our refuge.
Psalm 62:5-8

Submit yourselves, then, to God. Resist the devil, and he will flee
from you. Come near to God and he will come near to you. Wash

your hands, you sinners, and purify your hearts, you double-minded. Grieve, mourn and wail. Change your laughter to mourning and your joy to gloom. Humble yourselves before the Lord, and he will lift you up. *James 4:7-10*

If you obey my commands, you will remain in my love, just as I have obeyed my Father's commands and remain in his love. I have told you this so that my joy may be in you and that your joy may be complete. *John 15:10-11*

Pride

Pride goes before destruction, a haughty spirit before a fall. *Proverbs 16:18*

God opposes the proud and gives grace to the humble. *James 4:6*

When pride comes, then comes disgrace, but with humility comes wisdom. *Proverbs 11:2*

Pride only breeds quarrels, but wisdom is found in those who take advice. *Proverbs 13:10*

The LORD detests all the proud of heart. Be sure of this: They will not go unpunished. *Proverbs 16:5*

Before his downfall a man's heart is proud, but humility comes before honor. *Proverbs 18:12*

A man's pride brings him low, but a man of lowly spirit gains honor. *Proverbs 29:23*

For everyone who exalts himself will be humbled, and he who humbles himself will be exalted. *Luke 14:11*

You did it in secret, but I will do this thing in broad daylight before all Israel. *Samuel 12:12*

Do nothing out of selfish ambition or vain conceits, but in humility consider others better than yourselves. *Philippians 2:3*

Pride only breeds quarrels, but wisdom is found in those who take advice. *Proverbs 13:10*

The LORD is close to the brokenhearted and saves those who are crushed in spirit. *Psalms 34:18*

Deceit

Be self-controlled and alert.
Your enemy the devil prowls around like a roaring lion
looking for someone to devour.
1 Peter 5:8

Save me, O LORD, from lying lips, and from deceitful tongues.
Psalm 120:2

The hand of the diligent shall bear rule: but the slothful shall be under tribute. *Proverbs 12:24 (KJV)*

The heart is deceitful above all things and desperately wicked, who can know it. *Jeremiah 17:9*

They conceive mischief, and bring forth vanity, and their belly prepareth deceit. *Job 15:35 (KJV)*

The LORD will abhor the bloody and deceitful [rĕmiyahi] man." *Psalms 5:6 (KJV)*

The woman said to the serpent, "We may eat fruit from the trees in the garden, but God did say, 'You must not eat fruit from the tree that is in the middle of the garden, and you must not touch it, or you will die.'" "You will not certainly die," the serpent said to the woman. "For God knows that when you eat from it your eyes will be opened, and you will be like God, knowing good and evil." *Genesis 3*

"For I know the plans I have for you," declares the LORD, "plans to prosper you and not to harm you, plans to give you hope and a future." *Jeremiah 29:11*

Therefore confess your sins to each other and pray for each other so that you may be healed. *James 5:15*

Love

Herein is love, not that we loved God, but that he loved us, and sent his Son to be the propitiation for our sins. Beloved, if God so loved us, we ought also to love one another. *1 John 4:10-11*

If you obey my commands, you will remain in my love, just as I have obeyed my Father's commands and remain in his love. *John 15:10*

Whoever has my commands and obeys them, he is the one who loves me. *John 14:21*

He who does not love me will not obey my teaching. *John 14:25*

He knows you intimately

But the very hairs of your head are all numbered. *Matthew 10:30*

The LORD knows the thoughts of man. *Psalm 94:11*

Before I formed you in the womb I knew you, before you were born I set you apart; I appointed you as a prophet to the nations. *Jeremiah 1:5*

He thinks you're beautiful

For everything God created is good, and nothing is to be rejected if it is received with thanksgiving. *1 Timothy 4:4*

He has made everything beautiful in its time. *Ecclesiastes 3:11*

God saw all that he had made, and it was very good. *Genesis 1:31*

He delights in you

The LORD detests lying lips, but he delights in men who are truthful. *Proverbs 12:22*

The Lord takes pleasure in those who fear him, in those who hope in his steadfast love. *Psalm 147:11*

He will fight for you

The LORD will fight for you; you need only to be still. *Exodus 14:14*

He forgives you

If we confess our sins, he is faithful and just to forgive us our sins, and to cleanse us from all unrighteousness *1 John 1:9*

In him we have redemption through his blood, the forgiveness of sins, in accordance with the riches of God's grace. *Ephesians 1:7*

He wants the best for you

"For I know the plans I have for you," declares the LORD, "plans to prosper you and not to harm you, plans to give you hope and a future." *Jeremiah 29:11*

He listens to you

The Lord sees the good people and listens to their prayers. *1 Peter 3:12*

He sent His son to die for you

For God so loved the world that he gave his one and only Son, that whoever believes in him shall not perish but have eternal life. *John 3:16*

He who did not spare his own Son, but gave him up for us all — how will he not also, along with him, graciously give us all things? *Romans 8:32*

He sees and appreciates you

The Lord your God is in your midst, a mighty one who will save; he will rejoice over you with gladness. *Zephaniah 3:17*

How amazing are your thoughts concerning me. *Psalm 139:17*

He protects you

Call upon Me in the day of trouble; I will deliver you, and you will honor Me. *Psalm 50:15*

For he will command his angels concerning you to guard you in all your ways. *Psalm 91:11*

He offers gifts to you

I give them eternal life, and they shall never perish; no one can snatch them out of my hand. *John 10:28*

If you, then, though you are evil, know how to give good gifts to your children, how much more will your Father in heaven give good gifts to those who ask him! *Matthew 7:11*

He wants to give you the desires of your heart

Delight yourself in the LORD and he will give you the desires of your heart. *Psalm 37:4*

He fulfills the desires of those who fear him; he hears their cry and saves them. *Psalm 145:19*

He enjoys your singing and dancing

Let the word of Christ dwell in you richly as you teach and admonish one another with all wisdom, and as you sing psalms, hymns and spiritual songs with gratitude in your hearts to God. *Colossians 3:16*

Speak to one another with psalms, hymns and spiritual songs. Sing and make music in your heart to the Lord. *Ephesians 5:19*

Let them praise his name with dancing and make music to him with tambourine and harp. *Psalms 149:3*

Praise him with tambourine and dancing, praise him with the strings and flute *Psalm 150:4*

He's patient with you

The Lord is not slow in keeping His promise, as some understand slowness. He is patient with you, not wanting anyone to perish, but everyone to come to repentance. *2 Peter 3:9*

He will never leave you

Let us hold unswerving to the hope we profess, for He who promised is faithful. *Hebrews 10:23*

He is jealous for you

I am jealous for you with a godly jealousy. I promised you to one husband, to Christ, so that I might present you as a pure virgin to him. *2 Corinthians 11:2*

He loves you no matter what you do, or have done

For I am convinced that neither death nor life, neither angels nor demons, neither the present nor the future, nor any powers, neither height nor depth, nor anything else in all creation, will be able to separate us from the love of God that is in Christ Jesus our Lord. *Romans 8:38-39*

Other resources

You can find all these resources and more at EntangledBook.com.

Made in United States
Orlando, FL
23 January 2023